Paul Lengrand both as a theorist and practitioner in adult education and as a member of the UNESCO Secretariat since 1948 has written widely on life-long education.

AN INTRODUCTION TO LIFELONG EDUCATION

aside; good and honest people will come into their own, put an end to corruption and govern the *res publica* conscientiously and with dedication. Justice will reign between individuals and between groups by virtue of new laws and new social relationships.

Experience and reflection upon that period were soon to lead us into new paths of thought and action. None of us, indeed, doubted or could ever have doubted the important and fundamental role of political action. It provided the power and the means to overcome the forces of resistance, and when we look back at the most significant and valuable advances made by modern civilisation, we are forced to admit that they result, not from wisdom and reason, but from the interplay of political interests and ambitions, demands and rebellions.

A certain number of us were rapidly induced to change course, however. While they still recognized the crucial importance of the forces at work in political attitudes and operations, they were obliged to take other factors into account in their perspective on the building of a better world. That perspective was now one of education, and more especially adult education.

We can probably all sympathise with such a change of outlook. Political action requires simplifications. It avoids the finer shades and does not go in for subtleties. There are the objectives to be reached and according to what those objectives are, so people take sides, are friends or enemies, virtuous or villainous. Such a state of affairs is perhaps necessary and in any case inevitable. There are many people, perhaps the majority of mankind, who find this compartmentalisation quite reassuring, but this was not the case with us. We could not help being aware of the complexity of human nature, the many contradictions, the mixture of reason and unreason, generosity and selfishness which goes into the make-up of every individual, whichever side he is on. The imperatives of the struggle might force us to take no notice of our true feelings for a while but they reappear with all their original force as soon as the opportunity arises.

It was perhaps because we had this kind of temperament, responsive both to the differences and to the universality of the human condition, that we gradually came to set ourselves objectives other than the objectives of the political struggle. Let us call it concern for the long

6

IN SEARCH OF LIFELONG EDUCATION

What did we expect of life when we were twenty? We wanted, first of all, a life in the full sense, one which not only brought us the satisfactions of living but also offered the opportunity to advance as far as possible along the path of knowledge, feeling, art and poetry. We expected much more than this, however. We wanted a chance to contribute to the making of a better world, better for us, better for others and for mankind as a whole — how, indeed, could these aspirations be separated, since it is neither desirable nor admissible, nor even realistic to create a haven of peace and joy for oneself when the rest of the world is dominated by fear and tyranny? The events which followed were unfortunately to prove us right.

These were the 'thirties and civilisation was already at crisis point, showing incidentally that the crisis we hear so much about today is not new.

We were in an extraordinary dilemma. On the one hand, we were unable to identify with a society whose *raisons d'être* and values we could not accept; on the other hand, an even worse alternative, the triumph of racialism and other forms of irrationality, and a return to barbarism had somehow to be avoided. For this reason, we could not stand aloof from the great battles which were looming ahead.

Our recipe for improving the structures and conditions of individual and social life was determinedly (and for many people exclusively) political. We thought of situations and problems in terms of power and more specifically in terms of the assumption of power. Since the obstacles lay in the structures and institutions of an outdated society where disorder and privilege were rife, the only solution we could see was to change society.

At that age, one imagines that everything will come right if only one can change the system and the institutions and alter the nature of government: the villains will be chased out and the incompetent swept

5

This study, which was issued as a feature of International Education Year, is intended not only for education specialists but for the general public at large, for whom the future of education has become an ever-present concern.

FOREWORD

Lifelong education is a subject which is exercising many minds, sustaining much conversation and debate, and earning a high priority in statesmen's speeches. What are its fields of application and its significance? Can it be used effectively as a tool for analysis and as a guide to action? These are some of the questions to which the following pages seek to find partial answers. This study is called an 'introduction' deliberately, for in the present level of achievement and thinking none may claim to do more than to introduce a concept and to offer avenues for thought.

The book is in two parts. In the first, the author tries to show the logical and organic development of lifelong education in its various stages. He begins by identifying a number of challenges for which it is important that men of our times should be intellectually, physically and emotionally equipped if they do not want to find themselves on the losing side. But it has never been sufficient to identify a problem, however important, in order to solve it. There must also be a clear consciousness of its nature; there must be men who reject, contest, aspire and take decisions — in other words, there must be forces. This paper describes some of the forces at work: their impact is the dynamic which alone can bring about change.

The study continues with a number of analyses of the significance, dimensions and objectives peculiar to lifelong education, and closes with proposed elements of a strategy for educational action. It lays stress on the necessity to link together, in both thought and achievement, the objectives and processes of education as applied to children, adolescents and adults.

The purpose of the second part is to demonstrate a number of propositions and to illustrate certain aspects of the previous section which call for further explanation.

PREFACE

The purpose of this study is to throw light on the varying significance of the concept of lifelong education, to show what forces militate in its favour, to explore its dimensions and to define its impact and consequences for the educational effort taken as a whole.

The study fitted naturally into the context of International Education Year since lifelong education was selected by the General Conference of Unesco at its fifteenth session as one of twelve major themes for thought and action proposed to Member States in connexion with the international year.

The author of the study, Paul Lengrand, is a theorist and practitioner in adult education and has contributed, both as a member of the Unesco Secretariat since 1948 and through personal research, to the formulation of the thesis of lifelong education. He has also been active in making them known.

The views expressed in the following pages are the author's own and do not necessarily reflect those of Unesco.

CONTENTS

First published 1975 by
Croom Helm Ltd
2-19 St. John's Road, London SW11

and

The Unesco Press
7 Place de Fontenoy, 75700 Paris

ISBN 92-3-101263-0 (The Unesco Press)
ISBN 0-85664-271-1 (Croom Helm Ltd)

Set by Red Lion Setters, London
Printed in the United Kingdom
by Biddles of Guildford

An Introduction to Lifelong Education

PAUL LENGRAND

CROOM HELM LONDON
THE UNESCO PRESS PARIS

term. However short a man's life may be, it is composed of numerous episodes and passes through many stages. It covers a certain length of time. We did not believe the ambition of a lifetime could be reduced to the attainment of a particular objective, however noble and vast it might be.

A final word about people's different temperaments, conceptions and outlooks. Some people concentrate their attention on the collective aspects of the human phenomenon. Their interest is monopolised by the masses, by the forces at work, by structures and institutions, and it is these that they consider important. The individual, in their view, tends to be absorbed into these vast patterns and constructs. Other people, on the contrary, are conscious primarily of human experience in its individual form. What interests them above all else is the single, unique, irreplaceable life-story of an individual, the awakening of a consciousness,the whole set of ways of thinking, feeling, and establishing relationships with himself and with the world which are peculiar to the individual, his own particular way of tackling and solving the problems he encounters both outside and within himself which is, and always will be, different from other people's ways.

In the final analysis, there is a natural division of functions between the approach which could be called sociological and the approach which, for want of a better term, might be called psychological or philosophical. It is obvious that neither of these approaches is inferior to the other and that each makes its own vital contribution to our knowledge of man. It is nonetheless true that the second approach is in a very special sense the approach of the educator, if one accepts that the aim of education is to form the kind, the body and the character. After all, where else do mind, body and character belong but within the restricted and yet limitless space of a particular individual in the context of his own being and becoming?

These considerations concerning different conceptions and interests would not in themselves have sufficed to set our feet firmly in the path of educational action if they had not coincided with the conclusions to which we were driven by the events of the times in which we were living. There have been quiet and peaceful periods in man's history, at least if we take the history of only certain particular parts of the world. For us of the western world, however, such has not been our lot.

The ten years between 1935 and 1945 will probably be counted as among the most eventful and significant in history. For that brief space of time, everything was at stake, the fate of individuals and the collective fate of nations and peoples alike. Even good and evil — as rarely happens in history — appeared clearly identified, sharply defined and separated: on the one hand the negation of two thousand years of efforts to bring mankind out of slavery and idolatry, on the other an alliance of men of all sorts and conditions, resolved to oppose the triumph of the Beast, the satanic alliance between folly, contempt for man and lust for power. Suffice it here to say that the combination of struggles and sacrifices, organisational might and technological innovation, and the fortunes of war tipped the balance at the end of these ten years in favour of what one must call Good when one thinks of what the fate and future of the world would have been had the other side won. In the first flush of victory and, in our case, of liberation, it seemed to many of our companions that the time had come to exploit to the full a situation which looked favourable for them to assume power, and that the major objective, which was to transform the institutions and structures, should take precedence over any other. The means by which control was to be seized were to depend on the kind of resistance encountered. Violence and dictatorship were naturally not ruled out, even if they were not systematically sought.

Why were we unable at the time to adopt this viewpoint? Today the reasons seem to us fairly clear and strong, but at the time things did not seem so clear. Rather we followed our instincts and we argued more from what we could not do than from what we could (among other things, we could not bring ourselves to share certain enthusiasms, certain transports of delight).

It did not appear obvious to us that the time was ripe for that radical change of régime, however desirable it might have seemed.

In fact, despite a number of not inconsiderable reforms and achievements and in spite of a steady increase of the national income

8

which has benefited many sections of society, the powers of decision are vested in an increasingly small number of persons who are less and less subject to any checks, whether it be in finance, industry or politics. Far from having advanced along the road of freedom and responsibility, our right to be consulted on everything which constitutes the essence of public life seems more circumscribed.

We had no idea at that time of the course which our society was to take between then and now. Others better equipped to read the future than ourselves were perhaps able to foresee the withering away of democratic institutions, morals and conceptions. Our 'wisdom' at the time was limited to thinking that the revolution was not going to take place straight away — not one of those cases where one can derive much satisfaction from having been right.

From there, however, we arrived at certain conclusions and choices which were different from those of the trade unions or political organisations, which thought that the workers and their allies had to be kept in a state of constant readiness for decisive battles and in a militant, almost military frame of mind.

As is well known, the military spirit, whatever its origins, has a predominant tendency towards simplification. It cannot abide discussion or subjective interpretation. It manifests itself on the intellectual level by orders and instructions. No latitude or flexibility is allowed except in the restricted field of tactics and manoeuvre. It is an affirmation of the spirit of dogmatism, with all the short-term advantages that it implies and all the long-term havoc it wreaks. Militants can expect of their leaders devotion and readiness to take decisions, but can scarcely hope for accurate information from them as to situations and motives.

For the personal reasons explained above, we found it difficult to enlist under these colours; but, above all, we did not believe that this was the path by which that better life upon which our expectations and hopes were centred could be reached.

We attributed only a strictly qualified value to the merits of the military spirit even if we could appreciate why it was necessary for the time being. When, however, the military spirit persists after the circumstances which called it forth have ceased to obtain, it then loses

9

all justification and becomes a postiviely adverse factor. It seemed to us that the leaders of the working class movement, while acting in all good faith and for reasons which were often noble, had not attempted to develop among the workers that free spirit of enquiry, that questioning, original outlook which is the hallmark both of the scientific attitude towards reality and action and of an adult conception of thought and existence. Inspired as they were by a mystical view of political action, their aim was regimentation of the masses, for which indoctrination is a natural prerequisite.

This being so, what was left for us to do in our special position as intellectuals from, to some extent, bourgeois backgrounds? We had, as they say, thrown in our lot with the people but we did not share, for better for worse, the condition of the working class, and although we had enjoyed initial educational advantages, we were often lacking in human experience. The choice was not an easy one. We could always have kept quiet and toed the line, joining and swelling the ranks of those who, by their daily activity, though beset by the greatest difficulties, defend the workers' interests inch by inch.

Such is the call of service. It has its own grandeur and its own justification, even if it has to be paid for dearly by sacrifices which involve more than just time and energy and even if it means losing a part of one's soul. Although it is certainly understandable why some have chosen this path, it is not surprising that there are some, too, who have had a rude awakening.

We did not have the courage to make this kind of sacrifice, nor did we think that this was the way to make the best use of our particular kind of ability and experience. We were educators by profession; this meant that twenty years of study, practice, meetings and contacts, reading and research had given us a certain ability in instructing, communicating ideas and acquiring languages of communication. Both by inclination and vocation, we had established and developed a constantly renewed dialogue and exchange with very varied milieux, and the war had given us, as it did so many intellectuals of our generation, the opportunity to live and work with people from social and working backgrounds very different from our own. With this preparation, we felt technically and morally ready to make our contribution to a kind of education in which this experience of exchange and communication among adults could be continued and deepened. When one has experienced and practised this kind of work, one acquires a taste for it which lasts the rest of one's life. But we had also begun to feel that the work of education among children and adolescents, however important and necessary, was only a kind of preparation and only an imperfect prefiguration of the real process of education, which only assumes its full meaning and scope when it takes place among equals, i.e. among people who have reached adulthood. We felt that the overall future of education was bound up with the establishment and functioning of this new order in training and education.

Circumstances favoured a venture of this kind: by a combination of the necessities and hazards of the struggle against the occupying forces, a particularly large group of young men found themselves all together in the south-eastern town where I was working at the time. They shared my outlook in varying degrees. Their origins and their educational, social and cultural backgrounds were diverse. There were fervent catholics and no less fervent communists, engineers, technicians, a few philosophers and a few literary people. Very few had already held a job and, apart from their particular experience of command and organisation, most of them were 'absolute beginners'.

All in all, they were a mixture of exceptional maturity and great naivety. It was, in fact, a time for discovering the world and oneself, a time of birth and rebirth which gave spirit, wings and imagination even to the least likely candidates for such an adventure and those most inclined by temperament to settle down comfortably within the system.

I believe that the vocation which most of them felt deep down was not really for education, but rather for technical matters and politics, as subsequent events proved. My purpose here, however, is not to write a history for which this is not the place. Suffice it to say that above and beyond their differences of background, job, interests, and philosophical and political creed, what united these young men was the fact that they had come into contact with education.

Most of them had taken part in the Resistance. They had acquired

11

there that Resistance spirit which left its indelible mark on all whom it touched. The word Resistance of course covers a variety of factors, feelings and interests which were sometimes in conflict. Those who had experienced it in all its fullness, however, had found in it two basic aspirations: towards innovation and towards human brotherhood. The taste for innovation was aroused by the impression that the world we had known was crumbling and that the traditional edifice of institutions, structures, beliefs, myths and relationships no longer had any sure foundation, not even in the minds and consciences of those who set themselves up as its guardians and defenders. It was perhaps an illusion but more a semi-illusion: although it is true that no new world had arisen to take its place, the old world has continued to deteriorate and to lose credibility. We have abundant evidence of this every day; particularly spectacular explosions occur from time to time, erupting through the cracks in the system and showing that a new spirit is everywhere preparing to emerge.

There was something which was not a semi-illusion, however, and this, in the words of one of them, was 'the meeting of men'. It is a long story fraught with significance and rich in episodes. To put it briefly, these young men on the threshold of their adult life had lived together for months on end. They had experienced spells of intense action in combat but also long weeks of inactivity and waiting. What happened then is what often happens in a situation of this kind. Individuals lifted out of the rut discover powers and abilities in themselves which routine or constraints had stifled and whose expression had been inhibited or repressed. New qualities then emerge in people hitherto dulled by their lives, temperaments assert themselves and vocations manifest themselves.

These three elements in combination — men with many and varied talents forming a team, an exhilarating historical setting, and a series of specific requests from active political and social circles — were to make possible an experiment in adult education almost unparalleled in France. I consider it one of my greatest good fortunes to have been associated with it and to have had a variety of responsiblities and functions. I was given the job of establishing and later running a workers' education centre, with premises in the trade union hall. Our

12

task was to help to train union leaders and, in a more general way, those destined to provide the leadership for the new structures of the society born of the Resistance. Our work thus had a very pronounced functional slant. It was imposed on us by circumstances and it also corresponded to a doctrine, a doctrine we had all to a greater or lesser degree worked out for ourselves during those recent years when we had had the time to think and, to a certain extent, to experiment. We had taken a close look at what had been previously achieved in so-called popular culture in France and were resolved to follow radically different paths.

It seemed to us that the weakness and consequently the fragility of most of the activities which had aroused the enthusiasm and energy of previous generations was largely due to errors of theory. Our predecessors had remained prisoners of a traditional conception of culture and were consequently doomed to fail. They thought of culture as a self-contained domain comprising the sum total of knowledge accumulated over the centuries and the sum total of experiences and achievements in the various sectors of science, art and literature. As it was a domain, one could enter it or remain outside. Once one entered, one could occupy more or less of its territory depending on chance, the type of education one had received, one's tastes and interests. Some specialised in history, others in geography, others again in mathematics, in literature, etc.

If one adopts this 'geographical' concept of culture, it is obvious that there is great inequality of opportunity for leading a 'cultured' life. There are the cultural rich and the cultural poor, the privileged and the victims, the initiates and the uninitiated; there are those who have had the benefit of a thorough school and university education and who have learned the methods and languages of communications, and those whose intellectual materials and tools are limited.

One can understand why under these circumstances, the educators who devoted themselves to the service of the people in successive generations had one major objective: to reduce inequality and open wide the doors and broaden the paths of access to culture. They thus set themselves up as the distributors of an elaborate and, to a greater or lesser extent, codified system of knowledge. It will not be difficult to

13

guess the reasons for, and the basis of, our critical attitude. Whilst acknowledging that their intentions were honourable and noble, we could see a number of mistakes and fallacies in this kind of approach: mistakes as to the nature of knowledge and culture and the fallacy of presenting specific models of cultural experience dating from a particular historical period as culture itself and in this particular case, imposing patterns of life, perception and sensibility elaborated over generations by the bourgéoisie on other sections of society. The latter either could not recognise themselves in the interpretations given them and thus remained on the sidelines or, if they happened to be allured and tempted by certain aspects could pick up nothing more than the crumbs from the great cultural feast. In a word, this attempt to introduce workers to culture was flawed in its very conception and was doomed to failure.

We were motivated by quite a different conception of culture and cultural life. We tried to cut out *a priori* references to a ready-made, cut-and-dried culture and were convinced that the only service an educator can do for anyone else, particularly an adult, is to give him the tools and put him in situations where, on the basis of his own station in society, his own daily experiences, struggles, successes and setbacks he is able to build up his own system of knowledge, to think things through on his own and, by degrees, to take possession of the various elements of his personality, fill them out and give them form and expression. In other words, the ability to communicate, to stand up for oneself and to participate in the common struggles becomes, according to this view, as important as the ability to learn, whether to satisfy curiosity or to increase the effectiveness of one's work or trade union or political activity. Thus we came to attribute to being, in all its aspects and in all its many dimensions, the paramount importance it deserves and to set the acquisition of culture in its rightful place, which is the purely relative one of becoming meaningful only when integrated into a living, fighting being and into a series of experiences of life, each one individual and unique.

How far did we go in applying these principles? We did not, of course, carry them to their conclusions. To establish a coherent system of methods would have needed much greater knowledge and ability

14

than we possessed. Nevertheless, throughout our experiment at the centre, we attempted to be as 'functional' as possible. Rich in our team's many talents and abilities, we carried out a study on the current and specific needs of the workers we were dealing with. They, of course, participated in this identification process. It was natural that they wanted to be taught about business management and labour law. We added to this a history of the working class movement which, as we know, is usually left out of school syllabuses. Where we perhaps showed most originality and imagination, however, was in the field of intellectual training. Thanks to team-work in which technicians, engineers, ordinary workers, professional teachers and some philosophy specialists took part, we elaborated a method to which we have the programmatic name of 'entraînement mental' – mental training, whether sport or vocational. For present purposes let us merely say that this method tried to develop certain habits and reflexes of intellectual activity, starting out from an analysis of the main mental operations involved in the various phases of mental activity and deliberately ignoring traditional divisions between the various subjects. Thus, to take just one example, and without going into details about the various parts of the training, the operation of classifying was thus illustrated and taught with the help of elements borrowed from current speech as much as from the organisation of work, or from the classification of the sciences. The essential thing was, and still is wherever this method continues to be used, to demonstrate the place, rôle and importance of the 'classification' operation in all walks of life, home and social life, by which to carry it out. It was thus an original combination of living logic and living rhetoric, closely bound and linked to the needs and circumstances of action. Needless to say, since this method will develop the individual's powers of judgement and reflection and since it is based on a philosophy of self-sufficiency, it has enemies as well as friends, particularly in political circles which, as they do not share this liking for intellectual independence, have greater confidence in the formal education and its traditions and methods for the training of minds.

Worker education proper was only part of our team's activity, however. A cultural centre was set up at the same time and this too, using different means and by other kinds of activity, tried to meet the needs of a developing culture, integrating the various elements contributing to modern society, beginning with the work of men and the various attainments of modern art. To establish a fruitful dialogue between the various departments as well as between teachers and taught, an inter-departmental centre was set up. An association was formed to co-ordinate the different parts of this work, which adopted the name of *Peuple et Culture*. The association soon found that its work met a national need and it was not long before the group forsook its provincial surroundings and, as they say, 'went up to Paris'. It has now been carrying on its activity in Paris with varying degrees of success for a quarter of a century, alongside other bodies concerned with popular culture but maintaining its originality of approach to problems and its inventiveness in the fields of theory and methods.

Over the years we issued a number of publications which have lost nothing of their vigour and relevance, in particular the manifesto of *Peuple et Culture* and a textbook on mental training. The institutions we established were short-lived, however. They could not survive when the spirit of the Resistance ran out, when certain political ultimatums were delivered and when the team, except for a hard core of militants who have settled in Paris and now work at national level, dispersed to return to their own interests.

The bulk of what I have accomplished in adult education since that time, in almost thirty years of practical experience and of thinking back on and forward from that experience, I owe to that *Peuple et Culture* experiment which provided each of us with a fund of ideas and lines of approach on which we are still largely drawing. I was personally unable to adopt the political courses of action chosen by my colleagues in the movement. I had to leave the team and subsequently began an international career which was interrupted only briefly for national activities. During that time, *Peuple et Culture* lived on and fought on. One could talk endlessly about the many and varied contributions made by this handful of men not only to popular culture but to the development of the country's intellectual life. It was within that circle, for example, that the concepts of cultural policy and of the

16

sociology of leisure, concepts so full of meaning and promise, came to maturity. *Peuple et Culture* has never ceased to play a pioneering rôle and to be in the forefront of the fight to create a culture for our times.

All the same, we are forced to admit that we have not succeeded in our undertaking and that our expectations have not been fulfilled. What was our ambition after all? As we said at the beginning, it was to help to make a better life, and for all the reasons we have set out, our hope lay in education. We staked our faith on education, but what is the position today in France and in most of the other countries which we have been able to study or about which we have verifiable information? We are, indeed, forced to admit that adult education still exists only in a rudimentary state.

Even the most optimistic observers of the educational scene in our countries have to admit that adult education cuts a poor figure both in itself and in comparison with the other sectors of education. Although all children go willy-nilly through the educational mill and the period of schooling is steadily getting longer, how many people, after their school days, however long, are over, continue to study, to educate themselves, to keep themselves regularly informed and to develop, by means of continuous, organised efforts, the skills, gifts and talents with which they set out? Although it is impossible to give even approximate figures given the great variety of 'unofficial' forms of education that have to be taken into account, one can say without fear of contradiction that such people represent a marginal fringe group in the community.

Of course, there are important areas of national life where one may note with satisfaction that progress has been made. This is true of vocational training. The rapid progress of technology and the resultant phenomena of geographical and social mobility and the threat of unemployment have produced a situation which is favourable for educational action. In this field, the demand for and supply of training continue to grow; furthermore, legislation, administrative measures and funds exist in this sector, thus making it possible to foresee that the gap between needs and resources will be narrowed in the relatively near future.

But what about the rest? What progress can we note in the training of the intellect and of the sensibility, in aesthetic and above all in political and social education? There are certain active nuclei whose work merits the closest attention; but what about the masses who are, in the final analysis, the ones who matter, the ones who make up a community, a people, a nation or a civilisation? It would be better not to dwell too long on the inertia and passivity one can see for fear of appearing too pessimistic and too unfair towards the remarkable things which are being accomplished in the various sectors. What is certain is that the bodies which are in charge of, or have assumed the responsibility for organising this aspect of the country's political and cultural life function sluggishly on the fringe of society and represent but a minor force in comparison to other structures of social life such as political parties, churches, trade unions, universities, professional associations and pressure groups.

What are the reasons for this weakness? How is it that adult education, in spite of its importance for individuals and society, has not managed to establish itself and take strong root in our countries? This is the vital question which those among us for whom ephemeral successes and small achievements are not enough have been unable to evade.

There is a great temptation to blame the apathy and sometimes even hostility of the public authorities. Indeed, this factor cannot be ignored, since all authorities are, by nature, distrustful of anything which might lead to what they call an unco-operative attitude, in other words a critical attitude and a lack of respect for the established order of things. Obviously, this factor must be neither ignored nor minimised but in an overall analysis of the problem it occupies a secondary place and plays a secondary rôle. To place responsibility for shortcomings on people who, by nature and by virtue of their functions, have no incentive or reason to change a situation which is, or so they think, favourable to them, is pointless and leads nowhere. The analysis must thus be taken further and we must look towards the 'interested parties' in the legal sense, i.e. towards the adults themselves. Here we are forced to a number of conclusions which lead on one from another. The first is that there is one essential reason why adult education fails to make its presence felt and why it lacks vigour — it does not correspond to a desire, or in any case to a determination. Child education has such an important place in national life everywhere in the world because it is a response to a universal aspiration. Every adult, whatever his degree of development and his level of awareness, knows and understands the importance of training and education for his children. The desire for more schools, more teachers and a wider access to education finds expression in demands of a political nature. The authorities, for their part, have confidence in the school as a source of wealth, as a factor for national stability and integration and as the essential upholder of right behaviour and right thinking; since public and private motivations thus coincide, school education is founded on a rock and has an irrepressible vitality. If the indifference of the authorities towards adult education is to be replaced by an active interest and if it is to be given adequate structures and institutions and sufficient human and financial resources, it must come to be demanded, if not by the whole of society, at least by important and influential sectors of it. There can be no vigorous and flourishing adult education until it is underpinned and supported by a collective will.

But we must carry this train of though further. Why is it that adults who, as individuals and members of different social groups, are in great need of knowledge, regular information, and training for their faculties of comprehension, feeling and communication, only want education for others, particularly for those in their charge, their children? Why do they turn away from anything that resembles an educative effort in their own direction? Why this coolness and frequently even hostility towards any educational enterprise? How can one avoid the obvious conclusion that, for the majority of them, their experience of education has not been a happy one?

In fact, we who are involved in adult education are led by our analyses and thoughts to conclude that the weakness of our enterprise is not fortuitous, nor is it due to some ill-defined lethargy or inertia to which humans fall prey when they reach adulthood; rather, it is the result of a series of frustrations, traumatic experiences and missed opportunites. It seems obvious that if an adult loses interest in his education and, apart from exceptional cases, turns aside from both the highways and by-ways of education, it is because at an impressionable age, in childhood or adolescence, he did not find what he wanted and expected in the type of education offered to him or imposed on him. We had to accept the obvious fact that once the pressures and obligations exerted by the authorities and the family or by the need to learn a trade were removed, only a small number of fanatics made any sustained effort to study and learn. What other conclusion can be drawn from all these observed facts if not that education as it now functions is on the wrong track and causes a wastage of energy, enthusiasm and resources almost without parallel in any other sector of national life except, of course, military programmes and prestige projects.

As adult educators, we could not but turn our eyes and our attention attention to education as a whole. It was a logical development of what we were doing; otherwise, we would have been condemning ourselves to accept an absurdity, that is to say, to finding ourselves confronted with adults who are traumatised, cut off from the normal sources of their creativity and alienated from the natural state of the mind and the heart which is to never stop questioning the world or seeking self-perfection. For some years, therefore, while still carrying on our specific work for adults, we have been more and more urgently drawn to consider the whole of education and the succession and interrelation of its various stages. When we speak of lifelong education, it is the unity and totality of the educational process which we have constantly in mind.

It will be seen that we by no means identify lifelong education with adult education as, to our regret, is so often done. Why, after all, invent a new name for something already well designated and identified by the term in use? Why add yet another term, albeit with different shades of meaning, to the already lengthy list of expressions such as popular education or culture, mass education, community development, basic education, etc. There is enough confusion already. What we mean by lifelong education is a series of very specific ideas, experiments and achievements, in other words, education in the full sense of the word, including all its aspects and dimensions, its uninterrupted development from the first moments of life to the very last and the close, organic interrelationship between the various points and successive phases in

20

its development.

This in no way means that adult education is losing ground and becoming less important; on the contrary, it thus acquires a heightened significance and prominence. Firstly, the more adults there are requiring education, the more naturally will they feel the need to form associations and to receive help and guidance from institutions and people specialising in this kind of activity. But this is not all: the success of every project carried out under the banner and following the path of lifelong education quite clearly depends on the existence of a vast network of educational and cultural facilities for adults. No reform of education at any given level A is in fact possible nor can it be envisaged unless education continues at level B, and so on. If individuals are left to their own devices once they leave school or university and do not find in their immediate environment the tools and structures for a living education adapted to life in its continual evolution, it is clear that there can be no escape from encyclopedism, i.e. the unavoidable although anti-educational and irrational need to stockpile knowledge and accumulate ready-made answers to questions which have never seriously been asked. It will be seen that the concept of lifelong education is circular: there can only be lifelong education worthy of the name if people receive in childhood a fair and rational education, based on life's needs and enlightened by the findings and data of sociology, psychology, and physical and mental hygiene; but an education of this kind cannot be achieved unless adult education itself is firmly established in peoples' minds and way of life and unless it has a solid institutional basis.

Even now, however, the contribution made by adult education to education as a whole is a decisive and irreplaceable one. As we have seen, it was in adult education, beginning with a series of analyses of the nature, circumstances and progress of the work in hand and of the obstacles encountered, that the theory and, to some extent, the practice of lifelong education were worked out and are continuing to be worked out. But adult education's programmes and activities have also made specific and direct contributions to the world of education. The real educational innovations of our time have been introduced in this field. It was here that group work replaced the exclusive use of formal lectures, lessons and exercises. Adult education, except where it is only a substitute for and complement to school education, shuns the idea of marks, positions, punishments and rewards and all that clutter from a bygone age which our schools still harbour. Education shows through here in its true light as a process of exchange and dialogue in which each participates and contributes according to what he is and to his specific acquirements and talents, not according to set patterns. There is no selection, which is a brutal and wasteful process, nor are there any examinations and certificates which distort the teaching process and impair the normal development of the personality through fear of failure. In adult education, there is no hierarchy of methods and it is no mere chance that the less orthodox methods of education, visual methods in particular, have long been accepted in adult education institutions. In a word, adult education, at least wherever it is given its head and does not have alien patterns imposed on it for professional, political or partisan reasons, is education in freedom, for freedom and by freedom.

The question nevertheless remains, how can such necessary changes be made? Where are the forces necessary to overcome obstacles and inertia? Is it not an unbreakable vicious circle, since those responsible for taking action on education are precisely the ones whose interest it is to see that it does not change, those who maintain the traditional patterns which have made them what they are and which bolster up their position and their prestige? We thus came down to the root of the problem and it is essentially a political one. Only an evolution in political thinking and a new view of the relationshiop between the authorities and the citizen, between the governing and the governed, between the administrators and those administered, can make it possible to set the objectives of a new kind of education and give the strength needed to put creative innovation in the place of retrograde tradition. This does not prevent us either from criticising or from seeking particular solutions to particular problems. In the long term, however, the only solution to the problem of a better life lies in a society imbued through and through with the principle of lifelong education and in an education closely bound up with the advances and achievements of society.

PART I
AN ATTEMPT AT A COMPREHENSIVE DISCUSSION

CHALLENGES THAT FACE MODERN MAN

Existence has always meant for man, for all men, a succession of challenges: advancing age, illness, the loss of a loved one; encounters, and the encounter above all others of man with woman or woman with man, the choice of a lifetime companion; wars and revolutions, which spare no generations in their sequence; the birth of a child; the mysteries of life and the enigmas of the universe; the significance of a life, the relation of a finite being to the infinite; an occupation, money to be found, taxes to be paid; competition; religious and political commitments; slavery and freedom, political, social and economic; dreams and realities.

Challenges are still with us and have lost nothing of their force, directness or insistence, although in each particular life or given community they arise in a different combination and obey a different order of priorities. But since the beginning of this century these fundamental factors of the condition of man have been supplemented, with increasing sharpness, by a series of new challenges which to a large extent modify the terms of individual or community fate, render the actions of men more complex and involved, and jeopardise the traditional patterns of explanation of the world and of action.

The most important among those new factors — most of them taking the form of challenges — would undoubtedly appear today to be the following.[1]

Acceleration of change

It is not a novelty to say, nor a discovery to proclaim, that the world is in a state of constant flux. In his own day the Greek poet-philosopher, Heraclitus, exclaimed: *'Panta rei'* (all things are flowing — B. Russell).

25

Indeed since all time the landscapes of life have altered and ideas, customs and concepts have changed, from one generation to another. The disputation between ancients and moderns is surely one of the contestants of history.

What is new, however, is the growing pace of change. Innovations which formerly called for sustained effort by several generations are now accomplished by one only. From decade to decade man is faced with a physical, intellectual and moral universe so vastly transformed that yesterday's interpretations no longer meet the need.

Moreover minds are often behindhand in their race with evolving structures.

The world no longer corresponds to the image that men had built up for themselves since childhood. It becomes incomprehensible to them, and before long hostile. To conceive the universe as it is and as it is becoming, both on the political and the physical plane, is a constant imperative if equilibrium is to be maintained between the realities of life and the perception of life which every individual must gain. Failing to make this effort, men become strangers to the setting in which they are forced to live. They do not recognise the features of their own existence and end up by no longer recognising themselves. Never before has it been so essential to acquire the agility and adaptability demanded in the interpretation of the shifting elements of this world.

Whatever stress is laid on any one of the factors of our evolving fate, these factors all have this common feature, that they bring education and educators face to face with questions and demands of such scope and variety as to disrupt the traditional edifice of didactic notions and methods. The techniques and structures built up by successive generations to transmit knowledge and the 'know-how' suited to each society from the older to the young, from father to son, have for the most part lost their efficacy; and this to such an extent that the rôle itself and the traditional functions of the educational process are now the subject of critical assessment and scrutiny, and that education is increasingly driven to seek new paths.

26

Demographic expansion

Rapid growth of population is one of the major problems which most countries now have to face. Among the first consequences is an obvious one of a quantitative nature: the demand for education is continually increasing, all the more in that the consciousness of a universal right to education, which is wholly justified, develops step by step with increasing numbers. Meanwhile the expectation of life is also extending rapidly. In some countries men and women reach and exceed an average age of 70 years, and even where expectancy is still much lower it is fast moving towards levels of 40, and soon 50, years of average life span thanks to the achievements of medicine.

Not only the volume of education, but also its function and almost its very nature, require change to meet the expansion of populations.

Whatever the speed and scale of achievement of traditional structures might be, schools, universities and institutes can no longer meet the strain. In the developing countries it will take many generations before the educational system can meet the needs of successive waves of children and youths. The work of education will have to be pursued well beyond the school-leaving age to ensure the spread of knowledge and the types of training that individuals and societies will increasingly require. Such action can indeed only be envisaged through large-scale recourse, beyond the traditional functions of education, to all the vast modern media for spreading knowledge and providing training.

Moreover the preservation and utilisation of natural resources can only be assured through heavy investments of knowledge and ability aimed at all the inhabitants of our planet.

If we accept the principle that the expansion of our species should be be made subject to rational criteria and to equilibrium between needs and available resources, it would seem that only education is in a position to apply effective and lasting solutions to a problem which affects the dignity of men and women as well as the terms of their survival.

Evolution of scientific knowledge and technology

Scientific progress and modifications in techniques are gradually affecting the totality of mankind. Attention has frequently been drawn to the high speed of change occurring in the technological field. An international group of experts met at Unesco Headquarters in July 1965 to examine problems concerned with the training of engineers. The participants found that discoveries and processes which, only ten or twenty years previously, were in the forefront of scientific progress, had in many cases already become obsolete. The vacuum tube had been succeeded by the transistor, which in its turn was being replaced by micro-circuits.

Hence, concluded these experts, if the object is to train engineers able to adjust themselves to the techniques of tomorrow, the main effort should bear on teaching pupils to learn, since they will have to learn throughout their lives. If this is true for engineers, it applies equally in the case of doctors, economists and, more generally of specialists in every discipline, whether cultural or scientific. Languages are no longer taught today as they were twenty years ago, and the processes of literary criticism have been completely revolutionised through recourse to characterology, sociology, phenomenalism and comparative literature in the study of writings, authors, schools and trends.

A man who does not keep up to date is condemned to be overtaken, and let it not be thought that this rule applies only to scholars or the higher technologists. In numberless sectors of industry or agriculture the need for constant renewal of concepts and techniques dominates at every level of production.

The threat of technological unemployment is in all countries a continuing concern for considerable fractions of the active population; it is also one of the main motivations of a whole sector of adult education.

The political challenge

Political reality is without doubt the dominating factor in the lives of increasingly large sections of the world's population.

Changes occurring in the world's social, economic and technological structures are matched by no less frequent modifications in the political structure of the *polis*. Except in a few privileged countries men reaching

28

the age of fifty today have known two or three wars, several revolutions and countless changes of régime. Of the 131 Member States of Unesco, over one-third only attained independence during the last fifteen years. It is hardly conceivable that the world as we know it should be destined to permanent stabilisation in all its current forms. From one year to the next, sometimes from one day to another, men of our present generations find themselves projected into a new kind of society involving different types of political, legal or social institutions, far-reaching changes in the structure of the socal classes, the emergence of a new governing class and the creation of new relationships between the citizen and the public powers.

Without doubt the vital political choices are only indirectly matters for education. The cleavage of society by the drive for progress and the urge for stability and the choice between justice and order is imposed upon the individual by factors which lie far beyond his hopes, affinities, likes and dislikes. The masters of the game are self-interest, passion, ideology, revolt and submission. And yet although education does not play a determining role in the march of events, it is called upon to participate in the preparation, the putting to use and the consequences of events in terms of the lives of groups and individuals.

One factor which emerges at the start is of a purely intellectual order: minds are frequently behindhand in relation to the volution of structures. But the matter does not stop there: changes on the political stage involve at an increasingly rapid pace modifications, sometimes fundamental, in the rôle and functions which individuals are called upon upon to play in so far as they are not mere spectators, however kinowledgeable and understanding.

Generally speaking the very content of the notion (and rôle) of a citizen is continually reopened to question. The nature and shapes of power, the number and hierarchy of freedoms, attitudes with respect to administration and government, are none of them fixed once and for all. It is unavoidable that concepts, attitudes, relations between governors and governed, should be the object of constant scrutiny leading to the taking of options and to positions which are not necessarily similar to those to which citizens were driven fifty, twenty or even ten years ago.

Changes occurring in the foundations and structures of the *polis* have as their result that citizens are called — and will increasingly be called — to new tasks and responsibilities which they can only undertake with the desired competence if they have received suitable training. Modern democracy in its political, social, economic and cultural aspects can only rest on solid foundations if a country has at its disposal increasing numbers of responsible leaders at all levels, capable of giving life and concrete substance to the theoretical structures of society. The trade-union secretary, co-operative manager, member of parliament, or town councillor can only fulfil the tasks inherent in his functions, with the required authority and abilities, if he is continuously learning; for the administration and operation of the complex structures of our societies leave less and less room for a frivolous or light-hearted approach.

This is true in general, but even more marked and to the point in the majority of countries belonging to the Third World, in which all political problems arise simultaneously and with exceptional sharpness. In many cases the issue is to build up the material, economic and cultural structures that can buttress states of recent birth whose foundations are necessarily fragile. A civic sense must be nurtured, often in the teeth of traditions which run counter to the concept of a modern state. If institutions are not to remain hollow shells, these countries must have at their disposal without undue delay leaders at the higher and intermediate levels able to assure the functioning of projects, administrations and services. That is the price of genuine and effective independence.

Countries having recently experienced a revolution not confined to a mere replacement of ministerial ranks but affecting the country's structures in their social and economic aspects encounter problems of a similar character. It is not enough to promulgate a new constitution, to install an administration of a new type: the main effort must be made made at the level of minds, *mores* and relations.

Information

Individuals and societies must also face the consequences of the formidable development of the mass media of communication. Through the press, but especially through radio and television, one and all are now associated with every important event in the world. Occurrences such as war, revolution, a party congress, an economic crisis, the death of an influential personage, etc., which quite recently only became known across frontiers after delays of several weeks or months, are now immediately perceived, indeed experienced, by viewers or listeners throughout the greater part of the world.

This situation has profound repercussions. We are witnessing the growth of a civilisation of a planetary character in which every man is concerned with every other, linked with the other in solidarity, whether he wishes it or not, except where obstacles of a political nature are placed in the path of the spread of news.

The positive aspects of this interchange are obvious. There is here a decisive contribution to the development of a civilisation of kinship. The brotherhood of men and the common character of a great part of the problems they face emerges steadily despite differences in situations and variety of circumstances. It is as yet too soon to identify and measure the countless implications of this phenomenon, but in the long term, international understanding and collaboration can only benefit.

Nevertheless information can only play a constructive rôle if it is accompanied by an intense and continuous process of training. The understanding, interpretation, assimilation and use of the messages and data received call on the part of each individual for an apprehension of language — visual as well as spoken or written — for practice in the reading of signs, and above all for the development of a critical sense and of the ability to choose. Choice is demanded at every stage, whether whether in arriving at a judgement concerning the importance and degree of truth or credibility of incoming news or in giving information its due place in relation to the other means by which the personality is helped to grow and strengthen.

Leisure

Another factor which tends to play a determining influence on the condition of a great many of the world's inhabitants is the increase in

31

leisure time, although this phenomenon is probably not as universal as the factors previously listed. Leisure in its modern form, scope and content is a product of industrial society. In traditional societies of the rural type leisure and work — or if one prefers, productive activities and entertainment — are in many cases closely linked. Thus among the Dogons, on the banks of the Niger, the peak periods of economic activity, the fishing and harvesting seasons, coincide exactly with times of festivities and ceremonies. The productive effort and enjoyment are inextricably mixed. Again, even in industrial societies, the distribution of leisure time among the different sectors of the population is far from even. Every degree of variety is found in between the university professor who enjoys six months' leave in the year and the worker on the land, whose life is unbroken toil. Only recently have industrial workers obtained, in many countries, the right to two, then three and finally four weeks' paid holiday. On the domestic plane, men and women are far from enjoying equal hours of leisure, and it has even been asserted that the leisure of some is in flat contradiction with the pleasures of others.

However this may be, more and more humans are able to benefit from a new dimension of time, and it is essential that they should make appropriate use of that time, in their own interest as well as in that of society considered as a whole.

We must, of course, insist strongly that builders of all types (architects, town-planners, etc.) and those who utilise their services, such as municipal and communal authorities, should engage in no building scheme without having first taken account of the basic needs of human beings both as individuals and as members of communities. The utmost efforts of educators and psychologists, however constructive they may be, will be brought to naught if children, young people and adults have no alternative, in satisfying their need for sociability, to the street, the bar or the nearest cinema.

Yet the main responsibility rests with the educators. The most lavish occasions and opportunities for acquiring culture may be offered, but all this treasure will remain meaningless and without effect if men do not hold the keys which give access to such wealth. Towns, the countryside, human beings themselves are filled with

32

messages which, at any moment of a life, could make every man's existence richer. But these messages must be deciphered, the languages of painting, music, poetry, science and of communication with others must be mastered.

This is the basic task of the educator in the matter of leisure, namely, to help humans to become more fully themselves by supplying them with the instruments of consciousness, thought and expression of thought as well as of feeling. Those who, through ill luck, lack of will or weariness, do not cross the threshold of the cultural adventure will not know how to make use of the free time placed at their disposal. They will become prey to boredom, and boredom is to the soul as perilous, as fatal an evil as is a virus to the organism.

The crisis in patterns of life and relationships

Patterns of life themselves have been shaken. In earlier centuries men found in their heritage from previous generations broadly acceptable solutions to the main problems with which they were faced in their own lives. Often they did not hesitate, so compulsive were these models; they simply chose between a certain number, a limited number, of types and formulas. Each age of man donned ready-designed clothes matching more or less exactly peculiarities of character, mentality and sensibility but allowing each individual to be the person he was expected to be. Relations between one generation and another, between rich and poor, landowner and proletarian, master and servant, man and woman and husband and wife were to a large extent codified. Ceremonies, *mores* and customs were all-powerful, and although they sometimes imposed burdensome or painful compulsions, by and large they allowed most men to fill the place to which they had been appointed.

None of this exists any more today; none of the traditional types of humans wrought over the centuries by a slow process of evolution now meets our new individual and social situations.

Nowadays all is in question. It would seem as if humanity had cut its moorings and launched out towards an immense adventure of which neither the field of operation nor the objectives to be gained can be perceived with precision. Traditional conjunctions, contexts, age itself are no longer relevant. When does one become adult? When does one cease to be a young woman? Half a century ago a woman of 30 to 40 years of age was on the threshold of old age. Today she begins to assert herself in her full maturity. We are all hard driven to identify ourselves in terms of the images of personality conveyed in books and tales of former times.

A father who seeks to model his conduct towards his sons and daughters on the pattern which governed his own upbringing is in danger of erring gravely. He will not even be listened to. And how even sharper is the difference between the image of woman one or two generations back and that which is emerging in the years we live in! How can woman succeed in finding her true self in this new welter of shapes made up of feminine sexuality, of the relationship of love, of social and professional personality, of novel assertions and self-questioning? How even more difficult is it for woman to identify herself with the image which the opposite sex, sometimes in good faith and with goodwill, seeks to impose upon her? There is a whole range of teachings — on relationships, on emotions, descent, partnership, fatherhood and motherhood — that must find its place in these new contexts.

The body

It would doubtless be giving proof of great *naïveté* to claim that man has had to wait until present times to discover the body and its powers. In the first place the body's presence is always felt and it is quick to remind us of its existence if it has been neglected. In addition, entire civilisations have given to everything that appertains to the physical in the human being the importance that is due to it, and have learnt to make use, in festivals and ceremonies, in dancing and in sexuality, of all the resources that the body provides for man to express his desires, his emotions, his relation to the universe and his need for aesthetic expression.

In past times in the western world, major civilisations found

34

themselves in natural harmony with this human dimension. But as the centuries succeeded one another this harmony was broken in many societies. A hiatus developed between what was called the body and what was called the soul. Unity of being was destroyed and those values which related to the soul became magnified at the expense of others. Human beings were soon confined, crushed in a tight network of taboos and prohibitions which gradually led to paralysis and to fearsome trauma. In many lands, especially in the West, human culture was for centuries deprived of its normal relationship with biology, physical expression and sexuality. In these circumstances it is not surprising that the body finally rebelled.

Taking advantage of a lessening of the barriers erected by ideologies and customs, and skilfully exploited by trades which find here a source of rich profit, physical realities have burst upon our daily life. The press, the hoardings, cinema and television screens, popular songs, are henceforward devoted, day in, day out, to the visual and auditory expression of physical existence, with a strong bias towards the expression of femininity. Constant emphasis is given in all these displays to everything relating to sexuality, which now tends to occupy a disproportionate place in the mental and physical universe of our contemporaries.

Whatever religious or philosophical positions we may hold, whatever our preferences or distastes, there is here a fact which constitutes a major challenge for the modern individual, society and civilisation. There has been nothing similar even in the quite recent past. What should the reaction be to the intrusion of this blatant and pressing reality in our world?

There is here both an opportunity and a threat: an opportunity to enrich being, to fill up the gaps caused by the disappearance of traditional elements of our culture. We may gain here a valuable means to living experience, to expression and communication. But there is also a grave threat to the balance of being to the extent that these new forces are not brought under discipline and that the riches they offer are not utilised. We have to deal with an ambiguous situation.

It is clear that education in all its forms has the primary responsibility for lessening the harmful effects of this phenomenon and for extracting from it everything that will help men to lead a more

35

harmonious and full life in great accord with the truths of being.

The crisis in ideologies

A fundamental crisis is manifest not only in the sphere of morals and relations between beings but also in the realm of thought. Our predecessors, whatever the ideology they clung to, had at their disposal an ample and well-nourished stock of replies to any questions they might ask themselves concerning the meaning of life, the principles of conduct, defects and virtues, merits and demerits, sin and its redemption, what should be done and not done, and necessary attachments and inevitable repulsions. Every society had its codes and scales of value, stoutly rooted on earth and in heaven. Parties and churches had little hesitation in issuing dogma, regulations and directives. He who by chance or choice became a Marxist, a Catholic or a Moslem found himself snugly safe in the bosom of his option and in the community of the faithful.

Today it is increasingly difficult and unconvincing to identify this type of faith. Doubtless there are still convinced Marxists, unshakable Christians, citizens wedded to their parties and convinced of the excellence of their beliefs. But even where positions are strongest, doubt has crept in — not necessarily destructive scepticism but constructive doubt and variety of interpretation. Less and less is there a single mode of belief. Certain historic congresses and councils, disputes and debates, the evolution of ideas and knowledge, and in part the erosion of doctrines, have everywhere introduced a taste for discussion. History as we live it brings us every day a fresh opinion or a contradictory point of view.

This agitation does not spare even those circles in which by tradition the visage of serenity and certainty was always apparent. How can the average individual member of our societies remain unaffected by such a transformation of the attitudes and bearing of his traditional mentors?

Every man is in fact faced with the same choice: either to adopt an attitude of resignation and surrender, watching the cauldron of doctrines and beliefs without great concern over their contradictions and changes of front; or on his own account to participate in research.

36

Clearly, the second solution is alone compatible with a full and whole-hearted acceptance of the condition of man.

For the right to be man is complemented by the duty to be man, and this means acceptance of responsibility: the obligation to be oneself; to be responsible for one's thoughts, judgements and emotions; to be responsible for what one accepts and what one refuses. How could it be otherwise at a time when there are a hundred ways of belonging to a spiritual, religious or philosophical community? In one sense, the modern individual is condemned to autonomy, obligated to freedom. This is a deeply uncomfortable situation, but a stirring one. It can only be sustained by one who is willing to pay the price; and the price is education — education which never ceases, which mobilises every capacity and every resource of being, whether from the intellect or from the heart and imagination.

To be, or rather to become, an adult in our times calls for the same passion and continuity, the same pertinacity as would the moulding of any work of creation, whether scientific or aesthetic. If one is to succeed in this endeavour it is on the foundation of the consciousness of its imperative character. No one henceforth can be a philosopher, a poet or a citizen by proxy.

THE FORCES AT WORK

Obstacles and resistances

Education in general, and teaching in particular, have a crystal-clear traditional function. Is it not established that we are all, first and foremost, heirs? To link the present with the past and succeeding generations, one with another, to convey to the young what their ancestors have thought, felt and created, not only for themselves but in a universal perspective, to maintain contact with the major creations of mind and man in the fields of poetry, music, architecture, painting or philosophy, to ensure the continuity of the treasure of wisdom and humanity accumulated through the ages — all this is essential, for we know too well to what depths of poverty of being and of expression are reduced those who have not received their share of this common heritage.

Yet this same heritage will only have value, meaning and a true impact if it is integrated with the experience of a developing person engrossed in the labours, undertakings and struggles which modern man must face in order to meet satisfactorily the totality of the challenges he faces. To help man to invent, to place him on the paths of imagination, of risk and of every kind of research, to make him accept the position that his beliefs, attitude and knowledge must constantly be placed in doubt — these constitute the second function of the educational process.

For these purposes education should be constantly renewed in terms of its particular objectives, of its content and methods, in such a way as to take due account of current transformations, of the new problems which arise and of the life prospects which await those involved in the different aspects of the educational quest.

Nevertheless it is clearly apparent that there are few human endeavours in which greater obstacles to progress are encountered than in education. Institutions noted for their stability, such as churches and

38

armies, have been in full flux for decades: national defence is nowadays seldom planned on the parade ground, but rather in the scientific laboratory.

In Rome, at the same moment when the assembled bishops of the world were debating the forms of ecclesiastical power with the Pope, simple priests took their place in the Protestant conclave and demanded the right to participate in decision-making.

Up to recent days, however, nothing similar had been witnessed in the realm of education, at least on those sectors concerned with the teaching of children and adolescents. It is true that teaching, as given nowadays in most countries having a modern structure, has made some advance since the days of the bitter surveys and sombre descriptions of Charles Dickens or Jules Vallès.

Children are no longer beaten, and there is greater skill in developing their intelligence. They are no longer required to learn by heart the names of the tributaries of Rhine or Thames. Light has also been thrown on curricula and methods. Yet the spirit and end-objectives of teaching have hardly altered at all except in a few countries in which a didactic revolution has resulted from political transformation. The general state of *mores* has made progress, and the techniques of teaching have benefited from several decisive victories of civilisation. But the instruments available to society for the instruction and training of its future citizens, the school and the university, still reveal, generation after generation, the same characteristics: fractional links with life, isolation from concrete realities, a rift between enjoyment and education and an absence of all dialogue or participation.

The obstacles are easily identified. We have already mentioned the burden of communication, which by its very weight acts as a brake. The difficulties of the undertaking are themselves an obstacle: education is concerned with innumerable aspects of the life of individuals, groups and peoples. Where education is concerned, everything comes into play: philosophy, for we must define the objectives and values to be taken into account; the relations between education and psychological data, both individual and collective; relations with the structures and functioning of societies; the cost of education and its yield; problems of administration; and lastly, the fundamental options relating to equality, efficacy, justice and so forth.

Given the complexity of the educational endeavour, it is almost impossible to act in full assurance of success, all the more since the results of any action in progress will often only become apparent in a distant future. Even countries best equipped to know, and to take decisions based upon knowledge and experience, hesitate before modifying a situation which, despite its defects and deficiencies, has the merit of existing firmly and in apparent order. With even stronger reason, countries less well equipped from the standpoint of scientific data, studies and research, understandably shrink from launching into adventures carrying such a heavy burden of risk. Caution prevails over logic and reason.

Another brake on innovation lies in a factor which nevertheless assures the solidity of the school system, namely the principle of compulsion. No one will dispute this principle; but it does act as an element of immobility. Why change, why seek to improve? Why search for formulas which might better meet the needs and hopes of developing human beings when each year the school receives its automatic intake of users? The play of supply and demand, which commands progress, is here absent.

Nor does the teaching profession, as now recruited and moulded, show much eagerness for imagination and invention. Teachers are never, at whatever level of teaching, and by definition, in a position to engage in dialogue. They do not have to justify themselves as between equals; having undergone examinations they move from a status of submission to one of full authority. From this standpoint there is nothing, in the world as it is, to equal the concentration of powers vested in the person of a teacher. He is the instructor, the moulder, and holds the privilege of age and knowledge. He is right by definition; he is judge, virtually without appeal, and executor. He distributes blame, punishment and rewards. We know well that it is not in this fashion that a man becomes adult or acquires possession of his true powers.

The emergence of wisdom, of knowledge of men and situations, in this world closed in upon itself, can only come through the happy chance when some teacher escapes and makes contact with the greater world, that in which resistance by men and things is encountered, in politics, art, civics — and in adult education.

For their part those in statutory or institutional authority have no
interest in change and do not desire change. The aim of institutions, on
behalf of the family or of the State, is that education should produce
conformity.

Most school and university systems existing today are perfectly
equipped to produce a type of individual who will assimilate collective
myths and terms of reference as revealed truths. What authority of
every kind fears most is the questioning spirit.

Factors of innovation

In these circumstances it is easy to understand that the necessary
changes and adaptations can only take place through the impact of
forces powerful enough to break resistance and overcome obstacles.
Four factors have in our times played a decisive role, and they continue
to act effectively. They are political revolutions, consumers'
contestation, development and its problems, and adult education.

Revolution

Among factors that contribute to innovation one that calls for
attention in the first place is the political factor. The revolutions that
have occurred in the past half-century have all, as is normal, taken the
form of breaks with the past. The past was taken to mean economic
and social structures, traditional hierarchies and so forth, and also
systems of ideas and points of reference. Naturally, education was a
weapon *par excellence* for combating traditional influences and for
creating mental structures, attitudes and patterns of behaviour that
would favour the new trend of history.

This indeed came to pass, more particularly in those countries which
substituted socialist regimes for capitalist or feudal ones. One of the
priority aims was to mould the individual in socialist society from the
standpoint of production and of safeguarding the new institutions and
concepts of life.

Thus in the Soviet Union, to take one example among others, the
content of curricula for children and adolescents is fundamentally

41

different from that of the curricula of pre-revolutionary times, and the cultural background itself has been deeply altered. Whereas under the traditional dispensations culture and labour were kept apart, labour has now assumed the place which belongs to it within the notion of culture, in other words, it occupies a central position. The same may be said of all forms of political and social commitment, the cultural content of which has also been recognised and suitably emphasised. A considerable step has been taken towards achieving unity of the factors which constitute and mould the people's intellectual and spiritual destiny.

Particular importance has been attached to adult education. This was historically logical, since there was no question of waiting for generations to grow up before the instruments of the new society were available. It was also logical in terms of the Soviet system, which stresses the utilisation of human resources and the equalisation of opportunities throughout the life span.

A movement has been launched which should gradually lead to an even more radical reform of educational theory.

Some countries have gone very far in the invention of new educational forms. An example is Yugoslavia, which shows as much imagination in the quest for solutions to educational problems as it does in the political field. The two are indeed closely linked. There are few societies in which educational objectives play so preponderant a part: they are present in the different manifestations of self-administration, in the decentralisation of powers, in the application of the principle of rotation of management personnel and so forth. Yugoslavia is also, to our knowledge, the first country to have adopted the principle of lifelong education viewed as a basic link between all the different sectors of education and as the foundation of the new educational laws.

Consumers' contestation

A further decisive contribution to progress in ideas and in the renewal of formulas was made in the last few years by the dissent of students. It is likely that without the emergence of this factor the need for a new departure would not have appeared as clearly as it has. As we all know, dissent on the part of those concerned is, in the last analysis, the

42

determining factor in any advance towards reason, justice and true order. This has been demonstrated in respect of labour, of women, of colonial populations, and of all other categories subjected to any form of domination, whether physical, economic, legal or cultural.

Events in recent years are too well known to call for elaborate treatment. It is enough here to recall the importance of a moment in history when contestation, which has been the leaven of progress in all vital areas of modern civilisation (the demands of workers, of women, of coloured people, of colonial areas), first entered the realm of education, until then fiercely bristling with instruments of defence.

A major breach had thus been pierced, through student action, in the battlement of educational conservatism; and through this breach flowed an irresistible torrent of long-standing issues, swelled by new issues and hastened by impatience and fresh hopes.

As has happened in cases of destitution, opression or injustice, the victims here ceased to be resigned to their fate. Those who still accept the defects and inadequacies of education as the outcome of a natural order of things are less and less numerous.

Admittedly there is great confusion and much that is abusive in the current agitation. Nevertheless student contestation represents a fundamental and vital expression of that fighting spirit without which not one of the necessary reforms can come to pass.

Development and its Problems

Yet another determining impulsion has come from the developing countries, and this is doubtless one of the major contributions of the latter to the common cause of all the countries of the world. Through their endeavours the developing countries will assist in building the solid foundations of a modern civilisation giving due place both to the global and collective interests of societies and to the natural and justifiable hopes of individuals.

When, after the close of the Second World War, the development problem emerged as a central priority, in the interests not only of the welfare of the poor countries but of stability and world peace, it became inevitable that the socially and economically less developed countries should turn towards the more favoured lands and seek their guidance as to what makes a country strong and wealthy. The briefest and most summary analysis soon revealed the importance of educational action. Generation after generation, education has brought forth men capable of imagination, qualified to organise, administer and govern in accordance with the rules of a modern state. Without education there is no knowledge, no competence, no spirit of enterprise, no marshalling of a people's energies. Accordingly every state upon attaining independence desired and gave priority to the creation of those institutions that appeared as the buttresses of development undertakings, namely schools and universities. During the past twenty years we have thus witnessed a spectacular extension of educational structures throughout the world.

The available figures reveal not only the will to progress and the energy of the countries engaged in this effort, but also the extent of international assistance; for the rapid advances made were facilitated, and in many cases rendered possible, through large-scale intervention by the rich countries providing aid either in bilateral or in multilateral form.

While it would be unjust and contrary to the facts to ignore this important external contribution to community development wherever it occurred, it remains true that it is through educational activity that the developing countries are gradually achieving independence. In recent years it has been due to the existence of schools and universities that key posts in industry, trade, public administration and teaching itself are filled by nationals and no longer by foreign incumbents.

Nevertheless, and in spite of this spectacular increase in numbers, education is far from having fulfilled the hopes that had been rested in it. In many cases, the returns from education, compared with other forms of investment, have proved largely negative. Teaching has proved incapable of reaching the objectives set for it, namely to mould individuals to the situations in which they are called upon to conduct their lives in a historical and geographical setting; to prepare them for the concrete tasks and responsibilities of a society in a state of development; to induce them to accept change; and to supply them with the intellectual, scientific and technical equipment which would permit them to take an active part in the evolution of structures, institutions, customs and mentalities.

In this group of countries even more than in others, the effect of the educational effort has been to subject minds to archaic and obsolete patterns of culture and civilisation. It is even true to say that in many cases and in a variety of forms education as it now operates has frequently proved an obstacle to development by reason of the gulf it has established between intellectual concepts, the training of minds and the formulation of individual and collective objectives on the one hand, and realities on the other.

This hiatus between quantitative development and qualitative backwardness brings us to the heart of the concern which is felt by all those — theorists, practitioners, administrators and statesmen — who expect education to serve the true interests of man, both materially and spiritually, from the twin standpoints of the individual and of society. They are led increasingly to criticise the inheritance of the past, a past which in large measure is not their own. Better armed than in the earliest days, they are gradually shaking off the paralysis of settled habits of thought and feeling, that is to say on the one hand respect and admiration for the undeniable achievements of the countries which preceded them and of which they hold the inheritance, but on the other a fear of the vacuum, more or less enduring, which the disappearance of traditional forces may bring about.

For it is a fact that the installation of a new form of education requires a volume of courage, of inventiveness, wisdom and ability which far exceeds what is required by other forms of large-scale human endeavour. But once the responsible circles have acquired the necessary capacities and skills, the work of renovation proceeds rapidly. It is sufficient to cast doubt upon one single basic element in the educational system, for example, concepts of culture, to undermine the whole edifice and to make it unavoidable that solutions should be found affecting the system as a whole.

At the present time not only cultural patterns are undergoing scrutiny, but structures, objectives, curricula and methods. In the Ivory Coast for example, a radical spirit of research and innovation governs the reconstruction of the educational system. Indonesia also has tackled the problem in an adventurous manner, while in Dahomey a university is being planned in which the traditional divisions (letters, law, science, medicine, etc.) will be ignored and in which, priorities having been identified, a form of interdisciplinary teaching will be built up on the basis of a series of projects.

Adult Education

As it evolved, adult education was led to stress more sharply its points of difference with traditional modes of education. But this affirmation of separateness did not emerge at once: in its beginnings, towards the middle of the nineteenth century, adult education was dominated by patterns, for there was no alternative. The great majority of learners were at that time workmen who depended entirely for their training upon public and private institutions, their managements and staffs; while teachers were themselves subject to traditional patterns of culture, points of reference and upbringing.

Generations of workers attended evening classes because they sought a means, through instruction, to attain better conditions of living and greater security, or because they wished to satisfy a desire for knowledge and understanding, or again because they had to acquire competitive weapons.

Unquestionably many of these adult learners benefited from the effort they made. They acquired instruction, they improved their situations and in one way or another set foot on those paths of modern civilisation which call for schooling — but at what a cost in disappointments, misunderstandings and bitterness! The more pioneer-minded of these men and women, the bolder and more open-hearted among them, ran headlong into the wall of cultural concepts. They discovered for themselves that instruction is a powerful instrument of assimilation and conformity. They refused to let themselves be assimilated by a culture of a bourgeois and conservative character which exalted the values of the past, of inheritance, order and security at the expense of those other values, struggle innovation and openness. They reacted to the danger of a disembodied culture which claimed objectivity and detachment while it was in fact the chosen instrument for the defence of the interests of the governing class. They rejected the myths and mystifications of a universal reason which was foreign to the circumstances and to the fight for recognition of rights and social justice.

46

Another cause of disenchantment for them was the operation of the educational system. The teaching they received was modelled on the traditional patterns of instruction as dispensed to children: one-way transmittal of knowledge, exercises, tasks, checking of the learning acquired, examinations and diplomas. There was no attempt at differential psychology, nothing but slavish adherence to the classical structures of apprenticeship.

It is against this background of intellectual, ideological, cultural and methodological structures that a new form of adult education gradually took shape, born and nurtured away from the traditional paths of school and university in peoples' colleges (e.g. Denmark), in organisations for mutual education, in workers' or co-operative educational institutions, in movements or associations for popular education, etc. Through the experience gained in these new-type institutions there arose little by little a novel form of educational relationship. The adult taking part in training or study activities ceased to be a pupil subject to external discipline and receiving knowledge from a foreign source. From being subjected to education — in principle, the situation of every learner — he became the instrument of his own education and resumed command of himself as an adult. This new individual became a person in the fullest sense of the term, endowed with his own psychological and sociological options, aware of his own individuality and engaged in a series of contests each having its particular objective: the contest for survival, the contest for knowledge, the contest for individual and collective advancement. Instead of being condemned to an inferior status in relation to an instructor who was his 'master', the adult pupil became a partner in a collective undertaking in which he was in a position both to take and to receive: receiving the substance of learning, he could give in exchange the irreplaceable wealth of his own manner of being a man and of accomplishing a man's destiny as worker, citizen or other entity engaged in any one of a multiplicity of situations and relationships. From that moment the emphasis was on being rather than on having, and on having only to the extent that resources feed and sustain the individual in meeting the requirements and succeeding stages of his own development.

The motive power behind this new-style education also differed

47

totally from that which governed the teaching of children, namely compulsion. Willing or unwilling, the child is compelled by law and by his parents to abandon games and distractions for the sake of activities of which the interest and attraction are not always clear to him. The result is a great solidity in scholastic institutions, but at the same time a degree of immobility and conservatism. Nothing of the sort now affects the adult. He may, of course, be subject to indirect constraints or pressures, some of an economic and others of a political character. But an adult is seldom driven by force to take his place on the school bench. As a general rule he will only sacrifice his leisure and take part in educational activities if driven by self-interest, if aware of the link between what is offered to him and his own ambitions, hopes, inquisitiveness and tastes. Where no such link exists the decision is soon made: the adult stands aloof, or if he should venture, will soon abandon the experiment.

This state of things carried with it a variety of consequences. In respect of adults, education is now compelled to invent, to innovate and to imagine. No curriculum can endure unless it takes into account, not universal and abstract man but the concrete individual in all his dimensions and needs. Hence the obligation upon those responsible for adult education to be on permanent watch, to practise constant self-instruction with particular attention to soundly based findings in the human sciences. Equally essential is it for each one of them to modify the teacher's traditional image and to accept the fact that he becomes an adult among other adults, with his own blend of knowledge and ignorance, of abilities and incapacities. A solid basis of humility of a scientific character, devoid of all arrogance, will permit the development of a form of new dialogue, of a form of education in which the teacher must give a great deal more, and in exchange receive a great deal more, than in any other educational situation.

The results achieved in this sector are of considerable value, not only with respect to the training and teaching of adults but in terms of the whole educational effort. It is to adult education that we owe, *inter alia*, the development of group dynamics, the use of audio-visual teaching methods and research on leisure.

It is also from this quarter that have emerged basic thoughts and proposals relating to lifelong education viewed as a principle of coherence and continuity. The most percipient experts and those most amenable to innovation have discovered that adult education would inevitably be thwarted in its progress if the earlier stage, the teaching of children and adolescents, remained in its present condition. Starting from the evident — but too often neglected — truth that 'the child is father of the man' they have studied the concepts and operation of educational structures and brought to light, on the one hand the lacunas and inadequacies, and on the other the types of reforms which are needed if the human being is to remain in a formative condition throughout his life, if he is to keep intact — or better, to develop — the creative powers which lie in every one of us and which any unifying and conformist system must atrophy, to varying degrees. These pathfinders, through their inquiries and suggestions and on the strength of the experience acquired, are in this way contributing effectively to the formulation of a new doctrine of education far more mindful of realities and of the truth of man than traditional doctrine.

THE SIGNIFICANCE OF LIFELONG EDUCATION

The totality of the challenges enumerated in the first chapter — some of them traditional or coterminous with the human condition, others relevant to this moment in history — together with the foregoing analysis (previous chapter) of the forces whose impact is aimed at innovation, throw light on the magnitude and complexity of the responsibilities and tasks of education. As thinking and experimentation proceed, there are emerging a number of considerations which may help in understanding the range and significance of the educational process.

The notion that a man can accomplish his life span with a given set of intellectual or technical luggage is fast disappearing. Under pressure from internal needs and as an answer to external demands, education is in the process of reaching its true significance, which is not the acquisition of a hoard of knowledge but the development of the individual, attaining increasing self-realisation as the result of successive experiences.

This being so, the current responsibilities of education may be defined as follows:

First, the setting into place of structures and methods that will assist a human being throughout his life span to maintain the continuity of his apprenticeship and training.

Second, to equip each individual to become in the highest and truest degree both the object and the instrument of his own development through the many forms of self-education.

Within this general framework the following factors deserve special attention.

Age and education

If it is agreed that the educational process must continue throughout the life of the individual, then it is impossible to argue that there is an age set aside for education. Nevertheless there may be periods in life when a particular effort in apprenticeship is required. Similarly there may be periods of existence more favourable to study than others.

There is no simple or ready-made answer to these questions. Without doubt certain abilities are vulnerable to the onset of age: it appears to have been demonstrated that beyond a certain age, some sectors of the memory lose their sharpness and elasticity; the absorption of certain branches of knowledge — for example mathematics or a foreign tongue — presents difficulties which in some cases prove insurmountable. The same applies to gaining skill in sports and games, especially where disciplines are involved which run more or less counter to natural motions and where only the suppleness of youth can serve. Instances are dancing, violin-playing and skiing, in all of which skills, reflexes and habits must be acquired at an early stage in life if a given degree of performance is to be attained.

These examples, which are familiar to us all and which would seem to indicate to the unthinking that there is a set age for learning, nevertheless conceal another truth, which is that access to many forms of physical and intellectual existence lies widely open at every stage of the life span.

The learning process is also a habit, and anyone who in his youth has mastered the drills of apprenticeship may at any time become an initiate and a practitioner of new abilities. Certain forms of activity indeed, far from degenerating, tend to improve steadily, on condition only that they are kept in constant use. This is true, for example, of the use of words both spoken and written, and more generally of all processes and actions in which judgement plays an important role.

But the fundamental and true nature of the subject does not lie here; for when we question the ability to learn, we do so in terms of a limited and in part erroneous concept of the educational process.

The prospects of instituting lifelong education, and the need for it, are to be judged not in relation to other people or to a given body of knowledge external to the pupil, but in relation to the personal development of a particular individual.

Nothing is more bewildering and frustrating than the traditional conceptions of culture which underlie most opinions relating to education. Culture in a given individual is not measured by plus or minus signs, by good marks and bad, awarded in terms of the volume and quality of the knowledge and know-how of another, or of a hypothetical average intellectual model. A man's culture is the sum total of the efforts and experiences through which he has become steadily more himself. These efforts and experiences, even if he shares them with thousands and millions of other human beings, are his own and relevant only to himself. One man will have greater facility, another will encounter difficulties in fulfilling himself. But such differences in no way affect the fundamental finding that culture only exists to the extent to which it has been lived and tested within the particular history of a man who is leading an existence, who is building a life, who is conscious of the universe and who takes part in its shaping by his own actions.

Viewed in this light any apprenticeship, research, study or other effort aimed at progress in understanding and in relations with others assumes its place and meaning in relation to a continuous constructive process in which education represents the indispensable instrument.

While the discipline of education has its place, as we have seen, throughout the life span, it becomes more necessary than ever at those critical moments which occur during the life of any individual.

The transition from one age to another — from childhood to adolescence (which itself has several stages), from adolescence to maturity in its various phases, from these to the third stage and finally to the closing period of life — raises problems on each occasion and may even precipitate crises. Each stage has its strengths and weaknesses, its advantages and defects, and in any event a specific content. In order that these moments of transition may acquire their full significance, in order that they should prove, not moments of disintegration but elements of progress on the road towards sharper consciousness, more secure knowledge and greater mastery over the self, a particular effort of education is required on each occasion, as if for a fresh entry into adolescence.

This educational effort must be made in terms of professional skill, psychology and philosophy; it involves choices, sacrifices and resolves

52

which themselves require a complex of training, information and disciplines all forming part of a broad and penetrating concept of life-long education.

In any event the educational process, if it is to be living and to serve the developing being, must stand in positive relationship to time, viewed as a constructive factor and in no way as a factor of destruction. Accordingly educators must spare no effort to resist any notion of ideas and *mores* as being immutable; they must strive not only to gain acceptance for change, but to foster by every means an intelligent and efficient participation in the various stages of change, whether this takes place within an individual or in the world to which he relates.

Young people and adults

While it is true that education is a continuous process, it is nevertheless a fact that the forms it takes are not identical for young people and for adults. Quite apart from differences in biological and psychical maturity, the status and circumstances of these two segments of the population vary substantially. There is obligation on the one hand and freedom on the other. The child is subjected to the adult world as personified by his parents or school authorities. He is not in a position to decide for himself and can neither choose what suits him best nor reject that for which he has no desire or taste. In the context of education he is a mere subject. The foundations, contents and methods of the various educational systems into which he is slotted are imposed from outside; others decide on his behalf what is good for him and what will prove useful later, 'when he grows up'.

Things are very different for the adult. Except in very particular circumstances, no outside authority attempts to compel him to study, to improve his mental equipment, to become a better citizen or a more knowledgeable and understanding head of family. For as long as he has not grasped that a specific benefit awaits him if he makes a particular effort in the professional, civic or cultural field, he will keep out. And when he has gone in, it is always open to him to withdraw.

In these circumstances adult education, and more generally any form of education which is not compulsory, including out-of-school instruction of the young, provides a favourable stage for innovation.

53

Programmes of this type are the origins of certain forms of education whose universal significance is now recognised, in particular group work, organised discussion, participation in productive activities, seminars and study courses, non-directional methods, the full use of audio-visual devices, etc. The future of education regarded in its entirety, and its capacity to renew itself, accordingly depend upon the development of adult education.

Lifelong education also emerges as a possible solution to one of the critical problems of our modern societies, namely that which arises in the relations between different generations. There is abundant proof that communication and exchanges between the young and their elders are in a poor state, to such a degree that in many cases the duologue between father and son or professor and pupil is virtually non-existent. And yet these exchanges are invaluable and indispensable both for the reciprocal enrichment of the individuals concerned and for the equilibrium of society.

In the last analysis the main responsibility for this state of crisis rests with the elders, since among other things they for their part were once young, whereas the young have never been adults. It is therefore up to the elders to make the major effort towards understanding, adaptation, renovation and imagination, without which communication will remain impossible.

Above all, the element of authority must rapidly shift from a basis of status and personality to one resting on competence and open-mindedness towards others.

In other words if the adult is to be merely heard, if his stock of knowledge or his directives are to reach the succeeding generation, he must himself be in a state of learning. The adult must pay the price of constant apprenticeship and progress, of unceasing questioning of himself, of his knowledge and experience, if he hopes to gain the attention he seeks. This would seem to be the only path leading to the re-establishment and lively pursuit of the duologue.

Method and content

'Learning to learn' is now a much-worn formula which has become tedious through constant abuse as representing the perfect solution. Yet it means exactly what it says. Henceforward in any learning process the stress can no longer be laid on a necessarily limited and arbitrarily fixed content; it must bear upon the ability to understand, to assimilate and analyse, to put order into the knowledge acquired, to handle with ease the relationship between the abstract and the concrete, between the general and the particular, to relate knowledge and action, and to co-ordinate training and information.

In a setting of lifelong education this is tantamount to equipping the human being with a method which will be at his disposal throughout the length of his intellectual and cultural journey. It implies that the essence of the educational activity — whether teaching in the strict sense or, more broadly, instruction and training — must aim at the acquisition of habits and reflexes, of capacities. Hence the emphasis which should be laid on gaining practice, by every means and in every sense of the term.

Here again experience acquired in the out-of-school context is instructive and helpful. Whether we are concerned with the training of the mind, the development of the body, relationships with others, initiation in spoken or written expression, the deciphering of various languages, introduction to music or the plastic arts, we find in out-of-school experience a wealth of achievement, experiment and research from which education in its totality could and should profit.

Training and selection

Development of lifelong education encounters a serious obstacle, that of selection. The situation is well known: through the operation of examinations and diplomas, a sorting-out takes place at the various stages of education, and even more sharply and definitively in its concluding phase, between the qualified and the unqualified, the 'elect' and the 'rejected' of the system. Failure and success are thus institutionalised in a manner which is generally irrevocable.

We are also well aware of the defects of a system which attaches undue weight to an ideology of merit. Under the shelter of merit new privileges are in fact created, even though they are better concealed

55

than in the past, when birth and wealth were the only criteria for success.

Under the existing system — in which moreover luck and chance play dominant roles — the quick-witted are privileged as against the slow in thought, the intellectual type has the advantage over other forms of human expression and other temperaments, the conformist over the innovator, children from elegant districts over those from slums.

Again, rejection resulting from failure in examination leads to an unreasonable wastage of society's resources and investments both in cash and in manpower. Nor can enough stress be laid on the damage and emotional shock caused by failure both to those who endure it and find themselves marginal beings and more generally to all those for whom the approach of an examination at every stage of schooling creates a particularly acute form of neurosis — which, as we are all aware, extends to the parents as well. Lastly, innovation and initiative in the matter of curricula and methods are strongly inhibited by the tyranny of the examination.

Nevertheless it is impossible not to take account of the obligations of selection, of the division of labour and of the distribution of tasks.

This issue lies at the centre of all thinking and action relating to lifelong education. How is the educational system to be maintained in an open condition? How, under the pressure of competition, can we reconcile the demands of industry, agriculture, administration (to say nothing of family ambitions) with the avowed objectives of equality of opportunity and of the harmonious development of the individual in accordance with his character, ambitions and aptitudes?

We are faced here with a knot of problems whose solution naturally concerns education itself, and within education, the teaching process, but also affects the spirit, structures and functioning of modern societies. What emerges clearly is that a broadening of the prospects open to men in the matter of study, qualification, training and professional improvement is an integral part of the necessary solution if we are to equalize opportunities in accordance with the principles of true and effective democracy.

Unity and coherence of the educational process

There is a striking contrast between the unitary character of an individual's personality and destiny, and the diversity of means used for his training. There would be no great danger in this if the various approaches corresponded to the different stages of a man's life and to the diverse replies he must give to different situations. This variety is indeed not only unavoidable but can lead to fortunate results.

The problem here, however, is that of the antithesis, which is often deep, between the individual's own trend and the guidance he receives. On the one hand we have the same man, thinking, acting, rejoicing or mourning, developing or losing ground. On the educational side, on the other hand, it is as if a collection of different individuals has been brought together by chance into one mould and required to reconcile as best they could demands which were frequently incompatible. In the teaching he receives at school, in the family, the factory, the training workshop or the trade union, the individual — producer, consumer and citizen — receives teaching, instruction and forms of training of which the objectives and results do not harmonise.

Lifelong education represents an effort to reconcile and harmonise these different stages of training in such a manner that the individual is no longer in conflict with himself. By laying stress on the unity, the all-roundness and the continuity of development of the personality, it leads to the formulation of curricula and instruments of education that create permanent communications between the needs and lessons of professional life, of cultural expression, of general development and of the various situations for and through which every individual completes and fulfils himself.

In this perspective an effort at systematisation cannot be avoided. But the notion of system is here used to indicate research aimed at giving coherence and clarity to the interlocking mechanisms and the interdependence of the different aspects and stages of the educational process viewed in its entirety. Although many elements of lifelong education exist already, either within the orbit of school and institutional education or at the level of out-of-school education, what is so far lacking is an overall view of the problem which would permit a

57

wise distribution of responsibilities and would assist the process of thinking out and preparing for a reform of structures, the need for which is in any event acknowledged. Since the Second World War there have been in various western countries up to a dozen attempts which have failed, while education has moved from change to change without finding either internal equilibrium or satisfactory answers to the demands of modern society. It doubtless proved impossible — and would be vain today — to seek answers to these questions without having recourse to a new concept of education in which account would be taken of the constant and universal need of human beings for training, instruction and progress.

In any such concept, in which education would find its place in every sector of existence and would continue throughout the course of the personality's development, a great number of the barriers which now separate, often hermetically, the various orders and stages of educational action would have to disappear, giving way to living and purposeful intercommunication. Education can from now onwards be viewed as a coherent structure of which each part is dependent upon the others and only has significance in relation to those others. If one part is missing, the rest of the structure loses its equilibrium and no other part is in a position to render the specific services for which it was created. We must therefore proceed to a series of harmonisations, both in the field of theory and in that of practical achievements.

CONTENTS, DIMENSIONS AND OBJECTIVES

It is thus apparent that lifelong education is not a mere prolongation of conventional education. It involves a number of approaches of a new kind to the vital elements in the existence of every individual, beginning with the very significance of that existence. It enables us to perceive a whole series of fundamental situations in which individuals appear under a new light; and it brings novel solutions to certain crucial problems affecting the destiny of persons and societies.

Education represents the conscious, deliberate and well-equipped aspect of that steady progression which is the law of all human beings. We should of course not over-estimate the place and function of education in the fulfilment of particular or collective destinies. Proper as it is to insist on the inescapable necessity of making this effort, it cannot be recalled too often that there are structures which favour and others which inhibit the flowering of personality. Physical destitution creates and maintains moral and intellectural destitution. Men living on the margin of subsistence are also living on the margin of humanity.

Working for the construction of a society that will assure to its citizens a broad and equitable share in both consumer goods and cultural resources is synonymous with working towards spiritual betterment. Only Utopians still lost in a falsely idealistic vision of civilisation can maintain that there is a separation between material and spiritual values. These values derive from the same noble ambition.

The elements of a policy of cultural development, and within the general framework of that policy of the corresponding strategy, are the following: to provide all inhabitants of a country with decent housing conditions enabling the family to play its full rôle in the home as well as its educational function; to develop productivity in such a way as to increase the income of every individual and to increase the opportunities for consumption and for the enjoyment of cultural benefits; to increase the number of physical and institutional structures

59

that favour the development of social interchange and every form of intercommunication; to set up in sufficient numbers museums, libraries and cultural centres; and to provide all the instruments of teaching — schools, institutes and universities — required to meet both the thirst for knowledge and the demand for skilled manpower.

Action in all its forms, not excluding political action, is thus the indispensable instrument for establishing structures that will mark the different stages of that conquest of self which is the very purpose of education. This being so, any attempt at setting political action in opposition to cultural experience is sterile and, in the last analysis, doomed to failure.

It is nevertheless true that another illusion would be to imagine that a transformation of material and social structures, even in a progressive sense, would suffice to meet all the demands of the personality. Political action has obligations to meet towards the fundamental principles which govern the latter. Ultimately, are not the only sound policy and the only sound administration those which, in their principles, objectives and methods, take full account of what has been termed by one familiar with the subject 'the human scale'?

The argument goes further. Even the best policy, one which goes nearest to meeting the desires of men of culture and of educators, has limited scope. It can, and doubtless must, create the framework within which individual destinies can find fulfilment in favourable circumstances. But it cannot, even under the guise of a cultural policy, claim to take the place of the particular and original effort, unique in direction and expression, which every man is compelled to undertake on his own account.

If, on the other hand, education is to be in a position to help men to live, then it must itself be alive. Many are dissuaded from treading its paths not only because it calls for effort, labour and much assiduity, but also because it has so far failed, with very few exceptions, to draw sustenance from living sources and to meet life's needs.

For nine persons out of ten education means school, an activity of a particular nature expressed in terms of curricula, methods and specialised staff — a world apart which can only be described in an epithet peculiar to itself, 'scholastic'. School is a parenthesis in life, with its entrances

60

and exits. On entry the pupil puts on the garb of the schoolboy, to be shed at the time of departure. We can understand why adults hesitate to play this game, and why the only ones who accept are those driven by need or obligation, generally of an economic or professional character.

If education is to play the part we have described throughout the life of the individual and in all the dimensions of the latter's existence, it is clear that the prime need is to draw it out of the school framework so that it occupies the totality of human activities, relating to leisure as well as work. Education is not an addendum to life imposed from outside. It is no more an asset to be gained than is culture. To use the language of philosophers, it lies not in the field of 'having' but in that of 'being'.

The individual at different stages of development and in varying circumstances is the true subject-matter of education. It is accordingly difficult, and perhaps impracticable, to give education its place in any precise way. We find it wherever there is a conscious effort to be made, an option to be taken, a spiritual hurdle to be overcome, a contact of an intellectual, emotional or aesthetic nature to be established. Nevertheless we can identify a number of priority situations in which educational action is particularly desirable. We find them sometimes in an individual context and sometimes in a collective context, but more generally astride the two.

The life span

The first and no doubt the basic difficulty lies in the relationship which man establishes with his own expectation of life. The transition from one age to another is always accompanied by crises and may even assume a convulsive character. According to the manner in which the individual accepts passage into a new phase of his existence, settles down into a new mode of life and continues to keep in contact with the world and with his fellow beings, so age will signify success or failure, wealth or poverty, joy or distress, wisdom or madness.

The mere passage of years has in itself no significance and does not automatically imply a condition of saturation. Here education is

61

all-powerful, for a man may be moulded and trained to follow the rhythm of his own development. One first victory is to not allow time to acquire a minus value but to regard it as a factor of enrichment. On this solid basis a man may explore the ever new fields open to him and gather the fresh harvests which lie before him. Another important element in this process is that of becoming aware of the beginning and ending of the stage of life one has reached.

Man and woman

The man/woman relationship leads to analogous thoughts. There is no situation which calls for so much preparation, so much intelligent and continuous effort — and there is none in which so much is left to improvisation and chance. A man desires or loves a woman — and because they come together, all appears to be settled: whereas all is at its beginning. *Ars amatoria* reaches far beyond the summary prescriptions of Ovid and his imitators. This is a fundamental and particularly tremulous part of the art of life, and as in every other part of that art, it calls for apprenticeship.

Cohabitation during a whole life, or even during a part of a life, entails a multiplicity of problems for the solution of which mutual attraction and affection are not enough. To say nothing of the indispensable sentimental education, each partner must learn to know — and accept — the other and his or her individual traits, as a representative of the opposite sex and as a specific social entity. One must realise that the emotional realtionship does not rule out the generally accepted laws of sociability and cannot develop satisfactorily except in a climate of friendship. It is worthy of note — and here we anticipate some comments to be made later — that in a successful partnership each of the two plays towards the other a positive rôle of educator at every level of the personality. The basis of this educational action, as that of any other, is of course reciprocal attention and interest in the diversity of forms of expression of human nature.

62

Parents and children

Similar problems arise in the relationship between parents and children. An illusion of the same type as that which can spoil relations between the couple is that it is enough to bring children into the world and to cherish them to have known and done for the best. Here again there must be a sentimental education, of a different nature but as exacting as in the previous case. Communication within the family is generally woven with incomprehension and misunderstanding. Traditional society did not waste time on subtlety: rituals and customs showed sufficiently clearly and firmly what paths to follow. The father, acting by definition and by convention, imposed respect, while the mother contributed the necessary modicum of warmth and understanding. These at least were the patterns that were generally accepted and only disowned in exceptional cases.

Today on the contrary it is recourse to beaten paths and accepted patterns that tends to be the exception. This is not an occasion for protest, but a problem that must be squarely faced. We have nowadays as many original and particular situations as there are family complexes. Each demands its own formula, which calls for imagination and invention as well as the use of the broadly recognised tenets of the human sciences. True authority and the ability to guide and help the young can only be won at the cost of an effort in understanding and a search a search of conscience.

The profession

It is hardly necessary to draw attention to the links which exist between education and the demands of the profession. This is an aspect of lifelong education which stands out very clearly and which is widely recognised. Individuals on their own account, undertakings in the interests of productivity, and society as a whole, for motives of both enlightened economics and social justice, all turn towards education as a means of improving professional qualifications. Innumerable forms of labour-promotion are practised in an increasing number of countries.

63

One element, however, is yet far from having been recognised either in theory or in practice, namely the close and organic link which exists between professional training and general education, or in other words the totality of the individual's educational needs in terms of his development. While a man's profession is no doubt the most important issue in his life, it still remains, in the educational context, at the periphery of his being. From this standpoint the necessary effort of thought and achievement must be directed towards greater integration.

For as long as culture is defined, offered and doled out in a literary, philosophical and artistic context, or as a range of activities appertaining almost exclusively to leisure time, so long will the worker have the utmost difficulty in situating the essentials of his thinking and ingenuity within a true system of values. It is therefore of the highest importance to attribute to the concept of work, both in theory and in fact, its true significance as a cultural activity in the deepest and truest sense of the term.

This naturally presupposes a policy of production in which the conditions and rewards of labour are not inhuman. It is possible in practice, using labour activities as a framework and point of departure, to lead the working man through appropriate methods to a broad and penetrating vision of the main features and problems of the society in which he exists. Moreover so-called general education, that is to say learning the use of the instruments of expression and of scientific knowledge, acquires its full significance and its strongest motivation when it prepares men to exercise their profession. With the prospect of increasing mobility of labour, the more education becomes generalised in the sense of the development of abilities and capacities, the greater will be its practical results.

Education for leisure

A similar need for education is apparent in the field of leisure. Much has already been written about the place of leisure in the life of individuals, groups and communities. A Regional Conference on Adult Education and Leisure in Contemporary Europe, held at Prague in April 1965, threw light upon the importance, rôle and functions of

64

education in the endeavour to assure that leisure should assist man in his development rather than prove harmful to him. One recommendation of this conference is of particular significance in this context:

'. . . adult education is made up of a complex of activities most of which take place during leisure, and . . . at the same time it offers a variety of means whereby the use of leisure time, in its totality, may contribute more fruitfully to the development and enrichment of the personality;

'. . . [account must be taken of] the variety of the [aspects and] functions of adult education and of cultural development, such as vocational and technical education, study for personal pleasure, the formation of judgement and a greater appreciation of the use of leisure, the dissemination of cultural achievement and the evaluation of forms of recreation . . . '.

It must, however, be stressed that the coexistence of leisure and work has to be thought out. One and the same man has to live through these two facets of existence, and the manner in which he reacts to either will have deep repercussions on the content of the other.

Artistic experience

While it is true that leisure time has no monopoly of the cultural experience of individuals, it is nevertheless within the framework of leisure that room is found for most of the activities that have as their object intellectual, moral or aesthetic development. A man may read, talk, stroll, broaden his vision of the universe and his understanding of its laws, go to the theatre or take up acting, make music, paint, sketch, listen to poetry and recite it; in any of these ways he can on the one hand occupy the free time that is allowed him usefully and agreeably, and on the other, more significantly, express the fundamental demands of his being. Here again inborn intelligence or responsiveness, or talent, are not enough. Intellectual or aesthetic expression is not content with improvisation: the dilettante will soon reach the limits of his powers of

65

expression, will become weary and will turn away from pursuits that only provide him with mediocre gains. Here again, as in every other walk of life, the price to be paid takes the form of work: to know, to express, to communicate require constant effort. There is no way of avoiding study and persistent application for one who aspires to acquire and master the languages and instruments proper to each intellectual discipline and to each art form.

Physical education and sport

'A world-wide social phenomenon whose roots ramify deeply into the young and adult lives of men and women – participation and spectacle, discipline and recreation, profession and education, health and culture – sport is no longer related to the whims of individual escapism. Henceforward it is closely linked – sometimes as cause, sometimes as effect or mere symptom, but always noteworthy – with the major problems upon whose solution the future of our civilisation depends: the higher proportion of young people in populations, urbanisation, community organisation in rapidly developing societies, the building of structures in states that have suddenly become independent, the use of leisure resulting from mechanisation of work or from underemployment....'

In these words Mr. René Maheu, Director-General of Unesco, defined the role of sport in contemporary life.[1] It could not be better stated that sport today knows neither geographical borders nor social stratification, that it attracts men of all trades and professions, that it provides an opportunity for healthy exercise at all ages and that having broken the bounds of an occupation reserved for specialists, it has acquired the dimensions of universal culture.

This is at the same time a claim that sport, with which are now associated all open-air activities, should take its due place in lifelong education. And this is to be understood in a twofold sense.

In the first place the view must be rejected that physical and sports training is only undertaken during a brief period of life. It is far too

66

often neglected at the primary-school stage, when circumstances are nevertheless favourable for psychological and physiological development; it is most frequently found in programmes at the secondary-school stage; and in certain countries it only plays a very minor role in the activities of apprentices and university students; while it disappears totally at the moment when the individual enters adult life. This episodic and secondary treatment of sport in the educational field is in dangerous contrast with the importance assumed by sport in all sectors of the community and in even breeding unhealthy attitudes among sports managers, the athletes themselves and the spectator masses.

This finding should lead us in the second place to achieve a better integration of sport and lifelong education as a whole, to release sport from its purely muscular function and from its cultural isolation, to mingle it more closely with intellectual, moral, artistic, social and civic activities. The very conception of lifelong education, humanist and harmonious, is here at stake; it commands the overall training of educators and the full installation of centres of popular culture in which, within the same precinct, will be found both the library and the sporting facilities.

Not only muscles and nerve, skill and a keen eye, are involved when we speak of physical education. As has been indicated in a recent issue of a pedagogical review, the key problem is that of living within one's body as an integral part and buttress of one's total personality. The body has its own language, which it is as important to master as the languages of the mind or of the heart — all of them indeed closely linked together and interdependent. To fight against the various forms of physical illiteracy is in fact one of the major objectives of lifelong education.

Mass communication media

Relations between individuals and the major modern media of mass communication, radio, television and the cinema raise very similar problems. There is no question here of taking up a position regarding

67

the respective and comparative merits of audio-visual messages as contrasted with the written word. What matters here is, first of all, to acknowledge the all-powerful nature of these media, and next, to become clearly and exactly aware of education's responsibilities towards the media. Only a retarded spirit sunk in a nostalgic and restrictive view of cultural life would deny the determining rôle that they play in assuring communication between men and the world, its events and ideas, and the highly diverse expressions of the human genius. For the first time in the world's history any individual at any point of the globe finds himself connected with the life of individuals in other continents and lands. The daily sustenance of hundreds of millions of listeners and viewers now includes Bach, Beethoven, Stravinsky, Armstrong, Shostakovich, Tagore, Shakespeare, Charlie Chaplin and Orson Wells — to pick out a few great names in music, literature and the theatre. For every citizen in the world, awareness of humanity is ceaselessly growing in volume and content.

Whatever reservations may be felt about these innovations — and there are many — they can only be taken into account if we acknowledge the vast and unique advantages of the media, while recognising that, as in the case of most of the important inventions which mark the history of civilisation, they cause disturbance as much as they bring benefit. Their content and message are deliberately ambiguous and appear under various guises. The impact of new images, notions and values, often contradictory, upon traditional cultures, may and often does have an explosive effect. Moreover, while it is true that the media can convey cultural messages, the mediocre and the bad jostle the good and frequently have the advantage in quantitative terms. There is an even more dangerous threat to which attention has often been drawn, namely that through their very power and attraction for the masses, radio and especially television tend to fill up the whole span set aside for leisure activities and thus to exclude occupations of more substance and commitment such as reading, social relationships and participation in active forms of usage of free time. These are only a few of the numerous evils which daily experience and repeated inquiries have revealed.

There is no doubt that the political authorities have both

responsibilities and powers of intervention to curb these damaging effects and to draw from the new facilities placed at our disposal all the benefits that can properly be expected from them. These authorities must, with all the necessary caution, take an interest in the content and value of broadcasts and programmes from the standpoint both of culture and mental health. Recent inquiries have revealed what mental and psychological damage can be done to young children and adolescents by programmes blending stupidity, phantasm, horror and violence. Nevertheless there is a limit to the powers of authority, either because it has itself to give heed to concerns which have little to do with culture, or because 'censorship' is not sufficiently enlightened.

In the final analysis the only effective filters are good judgement, good taste and the intellectual courage of the consumers of these cultural wares. Listeners and viewers must be encouraged and trained through painstaking and systematic education to exercise choice. They must become accustomed from childhood, from the family circle and the school, to choose; they must get into the habit of saying 'yes' to one type of programme and 'no' to another. Choice must also be brought to bear upon the amount of time devoted to this category of entertainment and information. The hardest and also the most essential apprenticeship of man at leisure is undoubtedly that of learning to give his true time rations to work and rest, to participation and solitude, to play and to study.

Education of the citizen

Lastly all due importance must be accorded, in any programme of lifelong education, to the training of citizens. By this term is meant man as a public entity at all levels of his commitment, whether to the nation, the community, the international fraternity, or various groups of a social character such as trade unions, co-operatives, associations for popular culture, women's clubs, etc. Viewed in this light, the need for training is universal. The links between education and democracy have often been stressed and illustrated. On the one hand the development of knowledge and understanding promotes the creation and

69

strengthening of democratic forms of power and administration; on the other, democracy can only flourish and operate normally if the country can rely in increasing numbers upon citizens who are interested in the *res publica*, whose judgement is informed and who are capable of undertaking responsibilities within the various structures and at the different levels of national life. The smooth working of the wheels and cogs of such a régime demand from every inhabitant in the land a regular and systematic effort at keeping informed, and beyond this, earnest and sustained study of the problems with which the nation is faced. How else could we hope that the voting will be consonant with the true interests of the country and that representatives will be chosen in the light of their capacities and of their attachment to the common cause?

Much as judgement and competence are needed in the ordinary citizen, they are even more essential, and at a higher degree, in all those who occupy responsible posts such as town councillor, trade-union secretary, co-operative manager, etc. Acceptance of any public office requires on the part of the individual concerned that he give proof of earnestness and become familiar with all the substance of his task. The alternative to such dedication is frivolousness, and, as a consequence, poor administration.

Again, the smooth operation of a modern democracy presupposes the emergence of a new type of politician and administrator. It is essential that those who govern, at whatever level, should cast off the character of sacredness which attaches, through traditions derived from the ancient past, to any person exercising power. It is well known that power tends to isolate and constantly to corrupt. A man holding power should therefore be particularly vigilant in fighting off the professional diseases that threaten a range of activity which is especially susceptible to them, both intellectually and morally. It is indeed through straight dealing, a natural approach and a devotion to truth that communication can be established between governors and governed. Education of the citizen requires above all that the man in the street should find in his leaders the image of democracy in thought and action, and also in ethics. Only at this price will he feel personally concerned in the problems of the *polis* and will he give intellectual and emotional support to the good working of public institutions.

This aspect of lifelong education assumes a priority character in the developing countries. Quite apart from the intense educational effort which must be directed towards the masses in order that they may shoulder their civic responsibilities and take an active part in the construction of the nation, there is an urgent need, which will indeed continue to be felt over many years, for the recruitment and training of managerial ranks, and this need is evident at all levels. Industry, agriculture, transport and public services must all rapidly find managers, foremen, specialised workers and accountants. Very particular attention must be given to the training of administrators capable of keeping the wheels of state moving, and in the first place of implementing the measures laid down in development plans. Failing an effort of training and qualification matching the level of these needs, the autonomy of these countries will remain a hollow formula and their economies will not reach the point of take-off within a measurable period.

SUGGESTIONS FOR A STRATEGY OF LIFELONG EDUCATION

There can be no question of proposing a pattern for lifelong education. Every country has its own structures, its traditions, its inhibitions and its facilities. Moreover, historical evolution is such that any given moment in a society's history one element assumes priority over all others. We may, for example, imagine – and this has actually occurred – that following a revolution, and for a long time thereafter, a country will devote its chief efforts to adult education, in the meantime leaving other aspects of the educational process more or less in abeyance. The relative scarcity of resources compels selection and sacrifice. This is particularly true of developing countries, where availabilities in terms of qualified manpower and materials are often as deficient as financial resources themselves. Nevertheless the obstacles which impede the realisation of ideal plans should not discourage countries from seeking practical solutions, following the main lines indicated by the principles of lifelong education, namely:

The need to assure continuity of education, in such a manner as to prevent the wearing away of knowledge.

The adaptation programmes and methods to the particular and original objectives of each community.

The moulding of human beings, at every level of education, towards a kind of life in which evolution, change and transformation can find a place.

A large-scale marshalling and use of all means of training and information, going beyond the traditional definitions and institutional limits imposed upon education.

The establishment of close links between various forms of action (technical, political, industrial, commercial, etc.) and the objectives of education.

72

Highly diverse formulae can be built upon these principles, taking account of differing aspects but all obeying the same imperative, that is to say to render education an instrument of living sustained by life's contributions and equipping men to face up to the tasks and responsibilities of their existence with success.

At the same time it has been thought useful to spell out below some suggestions of a general character which it is hoped might prove of service to those concerned in identifying their objectives and means of action.

Trends

The foregoing pages indicate the emergence of two major trends, one moving towards adults and the other towards children and adolescents. We add below a few reflections concerning the relation between literacy and lifelong education.

The trend towards adults

The action of non-governmental undertakings is decisive, not only because it is necessary to take ideological diversity and a variety of situations and interests into account, but also because the spirit of innovation and research can only have full play in a climate of independence and decentralisation. Thought and practice in the educational field have constantly benefited during recent generations from the contributions and achievements of a sector in which the forces of self-interest, supply and demand carry weight at all times.

Nevertheless the state cannot remain aloof from a sector which is of vital interest to the nation, and it has already begun to show its hand in a number of fields, even though on a scale which bears no relation to the importance of the problems to be solved. We have only to enumerate a few areas in which the State, in varying degrees and in a form adapted to each particular case, can and must intervene if adult education is to be given the required volume and efficacy.

Finance. In most countries adult education is still a poor relation. Finance made available to types of education external to the school

73

and the university amounts only to a very modest fraction of the monetary effort made by governments to meet the training needs of individuals. Every official statement declaring the value, importance and urgency of action in favour of adult education is belied year after year by budgetary evidence. There is of course no question of public authority shouldering the totality of the costs involved in popular education: this would be neither realistic from the standpoint of national resources, nor desirable if it is admitted that adults must contribute to their own education through a variety of initiatives, including that of sharing the cost. But the resources that individuals and associations can bring together are and will always be far below the magnitude of the objectives set up for education. Large-scale participation by the State is therefore unavoidable, either in the shape of direct investment where government intervention is called for, or indirectly through grants supporting the action of private organisations. This requires from public authority an understanding of a complex situation in which non-governmental bodies carry out tasks of a national character which the State could not undertake with equal competence and authority but for which it is bound to provide financial backing as solid as that provided for other types of educational activity.

Law and administration. The development of adult education meets with all kinds of obstacles deriving from the living conditions of a great part of the population — that part, indeed, which is most closely concerned with such development.

If the new societies which have been forecast are to be capable of taking heed of the fundamental needs of the human being, they will have to pay the closest possible attention to the educational needs, some of which have been identified in the foregoing pages.

In so far as the generality of structures is concerned, it will be agreed that the extremely low level of incomes in certain sectors of the industrial and agricultural population must confine the thoughts of the individuals concerned to matters of subsistence, and that in such circumstances it would be largely Utopian to suppose that individuals who can have no other horizon than that of the struggle for existence could be led on to the paths of cultural life. Short of hypocrisy it is

74

impossible to deny the fundamental thought that the struggle for culture, at the level both of individuals and of society considered as a whole, must be preceded by the struggle for development for wages and housing, for transport, for health, law and justice, and so forth.

These objectives of the new, modern societies are closely linked, especially if we consider that the installation of a new mode of life calls for the intelligent and competent participation of an ever increasing proportion of the population, and that this involves a great expansion in the number of educational undertakings, professions, civic and cultural.

Nevertheless, and without awaiting a radical recasting of the structures of society, it is feasible and desirable that there should in the near future be a substantial increase in measures of a legislative and administrative character designed to remove some of the obstacles mentioned above. These measures can be grouped under the following headings.

Participation of workers in the management of undertakings.
This priority objective has its political and economic aspects, but has also highly important educational implications. The introduction of participation is in itself calculated to develop the sense of responsibility (which is one of the major objectives of adult education) and at the same time to increase knowledge of the machinery of the undertaking and of the economy. Genuine participation is the key to an essential sector of modern man's culture, to the extent that it establishes a link between action and knowledge from the point of view of structures as well as motivation.

Adjustment of work time-tables. Educational and cultural activities are consumers of time. Except in a very few countries, work is so organised that the miner of the office worker is tied to a time-table which makes excessive demands upon him and is irrational. This is a complex problem having, beyond considerations of efficiency in productive and administrative operations, psychological and other aspects concerned with habits and behaviour. It is sufficiently important to deserve systematic study.

Action within the undertaking. Undertakings are ready to recognise

75

the need to renew the equipment used in production at regular intervals, as one of the measures falling within the normal reckoning of investment, productivity, etc. But pressure must be brought to bear upon them if they are to agree to admit that the refreshment of the staff's knowledge and technical capacity is as imperative a need as the economic drive. The further training of an engineer, technician or official is a form of enrichment of the collectivity, and it is neither fair nor efficient to leave it to the individuals to bear the costs. This is another problem which deserves close study under all its aspects and which should be the subject of legislative and administrative action.

Among necessary innovations, priority should be given to a type of measure which is already in force in a number of countries (mostly those with socialist régimes) aimed at including the hours spent on specified educational activities within the normal working time-table. It might also be envisaged that workers preparing for diplomas should benefit from a given number of days (or weeks) annually, to be granted in the period immediately preceding their examinations.

The State might give the example in introducing such measures in nationalised undertakings, for they provide an answer to the concern for greater equality of opportunities for promotion and access to culture, while at the same time fostering the demand for greater efficiency.

Equipment. Educational action is closely related to the policy of cultural development. While it is true that, as a result of the current transformation of minds and of teaching methods, stress must increasingly be laid on self-education, the fact remains that the adult must be assisted in his efforts at every stage of his educational progression by appropriate institutions continuously supplying the material and the stimulus that he needs.

Two solutions lie open: one is to create new institutions, as comprehensive in scope as possible and open to all sectors of the population: libraries and museums within easy reach of the users, cultural centres, vocational training schools, etc.; the other is to stimulate and facilitate the use for adult education purposes of existing structures such as schools, colleges and universities. Regarding the latter, nations have at their disposal a complex of means and resources which are largely wasted, in the absence of an over-all conception of educational action. Such a conception should heneceforward govern all school construction programmes, in the spirit which has inspired such achievements as the 'village colleges' in the United Kingdom or the educational and cultural centre at Yerres in France. The argument is still more valid when applied to the major communication media, radio and television, over which the State frequently exercises a quasi-monopoly and which, if competently used, constitute powerful instruments of training as well as information.

Services. Public authorities are in a position to render considerable services, and indeed some have already begun to do so, although on a minor scale. Apart from direct financial assistance, to which reference has been made above, these authorities can take effective action in two priority areas.

Training of staff. Experience and study show that adult education cannot follow the paths laid out by traditional teaching methods intended for children. Programmes designed for adults can only be carried through effectively and reach their objectives if those responsible for the work have undergone psychological, sociological, technical and educational training of a type specifically matching adults' motivations, their absorptive capacities and the demands of their development. These problems are of such magnitude and complexity as to exceed the powers of most private institutions. Only the State is in a position to meet requirements in an appropriate manner.

The way has already been shown in a few countries through the creation of national training institutes; but public authorities are frequently chiefly concerned with sport and physical education, sometimes to the detriment of other aspects of the training of young persons and adults.

Here again there is a need for co-ordination and harmonisation between the private and public sectors. While it is true that only the latter sector is able to mobilise means of action of sufficient magnitude, we should not for that reason disregard the essential, and indeed fundamental, contribution represented by the experience gained in popular education circles, always freer in their action and better placed to give expression to the desires of the adult population in all its diversity of types and needs.

Research. If training is to rest on sound foundations and to meet the needs of society and individuals, it is essential that it should constantly profit from the contribution of the human sciences. Here again the State, through its research institutions and through the universities, is better placed than private bodies to advance knowledge and to promote the use of the psychological, sociological, economic and statistical elements which come into play in this vast undertaking, the continuous education of the nation.

The trend towards children

Whatever the volume and depth of any campaign undertaken on behalf of adult education, success can only follow if equally resolute action is take to amend the structures, curricula and methods of the first stages of education, those designed for children and adolescents. For the chief agent of adult education is the adult himself, with on the one hand his leanings, capacities, hopes and motivations, and on the other obstacles, dead ends and bottle-necks of various sorts. At the same time as he is moulded by the life he leads, the adult is heir to the child he once was. The consequence is that if, in his early years, he received a type of training that made him turn away from study and progress, or that did not prepare him adequately for the type of persistence and effort that the continuity of the educational process calls for, he is in essence a lost cause in terms of adult education.

This is not the place to undertake a critical examination of the contents of the training currently being dispensed in schools and universities. It is sufficient to say that this training is based on archaic models constructed for the most part in terms of aristocratic societies; and that it has only been tinkered with since, without any attempt to test its spirit and methods in the light of the new objectives of modern societies. The deficiencies of such teaching are becoming clearer and clearer. We need only recall here what has been analysed at greater length elsewhere, namely that it rests upon a truncated concept of

78

personality: the capacity to acquire knowledge is given precedence over all other forms of expression, emotional, social, aesthetic or physical. No consideration is given to differences of character, and those pupils who do not conform to pattern become marginal, as do those whose development is slower than the average rate. The need for selection prevails over the demands of training. Failure is institutionalised at the cost of senseless wastage of intellectual and monetary investment. These are only a few of the more unhappy aspects of a range of systems which shows every sign of exhaustion. The time has come to give unceasing battle in order to arrive at a new form of education based on criteria of reason and efficiency, and so shaped as not to outrage human nature.

In relation to adult education, action of this type aiming at the reform of primary education has both advantages and drawbacks. The main advantage would be the creation of a vast complex of laws, regulations, constructions and teaching capacities at every grade. Yet the very magnitude of this complex represents an obstacle. How shall we alter solidly established traditions? How shall we change states of mind, professional and career interests? How shall we, for example, reconcile the demands of training and the need for selection? These are questions among others to which there is no ready answer nor quick solution. We are nevertheless faced henceforward with a crisis in education which, despite its negative aspects, allows a clear view of a number of avenues along which exploratory action can be taken with a view to founding the new order.

Personalisation of teaching. If education has meaning, it must enable every individual to develop in accordance with his own nature and as a function of his own leanings and capacities, not in terms of a ready-made model only suited to one particular type of subject, namely the 'gifted' pupil who learns easily and does not question the school order.

Accent on method. Accepting that all knowledge is of a relative character, we are led to concentrate attention, within the educational process, on the acquisition of the tools of knowledge and expression: language, spoken and written, mathematics, the media of artistic expression such as drawing, music, singing, dancing, and physical training.

79

The function of the school is, through systematic training, 'teaching to learn', by developing the capacities of reflection, of organising one's work, of establishing a relationship between analysis and synthesis, and by encouraging the habit of dialogue and of team-work.

From a methodological angle there should also be considered the prospect of establishing closer links between various disciplines with a view to harnessing together the scientific and the literary approaches. *Links with daily existence.* The task of education is to prepare tomorrow's adult to face the obligations and responsibilities of life, to accept change and all forms of intellectual and cultural adventure, and to adapt himself to rapid evolution in *mores* and doctrines. This implies the following objectives among others:

Inclusion of the values which appertain to labour among the themes of culture in modern life.

Some initiation into the workings of the law and of the economy, by way of explanation and introduction to a rational conception of structures and relations.

Initiation in the use of the major media of dissemination of knowledge and entertainment (film, radio, television).

Constant attention to reading (learning the language of poetry and of philosophy, the problem of fast reading, etc.).

Initiation into the art of living.

Discovery and assimilation of the values of human partnership in all its aspects (duologue, sexuality, complementing one another, etc.).

Literacy and lifelong education

Literacy teaching provides one of the best illustrations of the soundness of the concept of lifelong education. This statement requires interpretation, which is fully supported by the facts. Experience shows that where a literacy effort has succeeded, it has done so through being considered as a continuing factor in a global framework.

We shall not set out again here the principles of functional literacy teaching. It will be sufficient to recall that the system rests upon a close analysis of the inadequacies and failures of traditional types of literacy campaigns. In the past, and very often still today, the most frequent occurrence has been for illiterate adults to be taught the rudiments of reading, writing and arithmetic without regard to the social and economic circumstances of their lives and with no thought for the consequences and future use of the knowledge they have acquired, given the personality of each adult taken by himself. Such teaching was often based upon an abstract conception of man cut off from his deep motivations and reduced to a so-called cultural 'dimension' and to arbitrary notions of culture, justice and equality.

With functional literacy solid progress has been made towards meeting man in his concrete reality. The subject of the educational process now becomes the individual in his dimension as a producer, and this marks a tremendous step forward in the theory and practice of education as applied to literacy work. In the first place it implies an acknowledgement of the high priority value of work in any modern and realistic conception of culture. Work is thus recognised as one of the essential factors through which the world attains a human dimension.

An adult acquiring functional literacy is one called to take an active part in the transformation of the structures and living conditions of the world in which he has his place in terms of the general programmes of development of society and of the political objectives which are bound up with the building of the nation. He thus takes up a position within the effective reality of a collective evolution which both governs and sustains the demands of his own development as an individual.

Yet the definition and the promotion of the notion of functional literacy involves at the same time the development of certain new approaches and the casting aside of various obsolete prejudices and tenets. In contrast to what is often maintained, literacy is not necessarily the first stage in the educational process. It takes its place in a complex of actions and undertakings aimed at raising the level of consciousness in men and at supplying them with the intellectual equipment they will need in order to express themselves, to communicate, to become informed with precision and to penetrate the realms of modern science. Literacy is undoubtedly a privileged and irreplaceable instrument. Without mastery of reading and writing the paths that lead to study and to participation in cultural life are totally barred.

Contrary to a widespread belief, literacy is an instrument of a complex nature which, in relation to other means of transmitting thought or feeling — for example images or speech — lies at an unusually high level of abstraction. The utility of this particular medium as compared with others is not immediately apparent to those who stand to profit from it. Only in the light of an overall conception of adult education, resting upon an understanding of the channels of perception, of the recognition of signs and of the assimilation of messages, and only on the basis of a clear vision of the links and articulations existing between the various elements of the adult's intellectual and emotional experience, will it become possible to bring literacy teaching into play in the educational process, at the opportune moment and with the full impact of its significance. One cannot give too much weight to the notion that the value of literacy, like that of any other instrument, is only relative, and that literacy will only reach its full meaning and utility as part of a social, economic, political and also educational complex.

Acquiring literacy is neither solely nor basically the process of mastering a means of communication, nor does it imply the mere gaining of a new mode of expression. Its true meaning is the passage from one type of civilisation to another, or more explicitly, the passage from an oral civilisation, with its accompaniment of traditions and customs, to a written civilisation with its own assortment of references, innovations, transformations of the bases of legality, and introductions to rational processes of perception and reflection. It is at the same time the passage from a society closed in upon itself to one which is necessarily open to the world. Its consequences are very often incalculable, in the short term and assuredly so in the medium and long term.

The objectives and components of lifelong education accordingly have solid roots in all actions related to a functional view of literacy teaching, and this conclusion is highly favourable to the theses of lifelong education. Put in another way, if literacy is to fulfil its role fully and efficiently, it appears inevitable that it will build up even closer bonds and relations with the theory and practice of lifelong education as applied to adults.

Short- and long-term objectives

In the long term it is more and more clearly apparent that lifelong education presupposes a recasting of the totality of the educational system along lines of thought and action of which an outline has been given in the preceding chapters. This task will occupy much time, the final objective being a more efficient and more open society in which man, his dimensions and aspirations, will receive greater respect.

It is, however, impossible to wait until all the preconditions for such a society are present before taking action, bearing in mind that the realisation of all these pre-conditions at the same moment is most unlikely.

Now is the time therefore for taking a variety of measures meeting immediate needs and tending to favour the evolution of the system in the direction of structures assuring lifelong education.

In the short term a rational education policy might set itself the following objectives.

Development of adult education

1. This meets the educational needs which emerge from the list of challenges enumerated in the first chapter.
2. Failing an elaborate network of structures for adult education, no serious reform of school education is possible, because of the need to supply the pupils with learning of an encyclopaedic nature.
3. Adult education provides a unique laboratory for finalising the structures and methods of a type of education not subject to traditional patterns.
4. To the extent that it transforms the mentality and behaviour patterns of its subjects, adult education exerts a fundamental influence on individuals who themelves have a determining voice in the educational field, namely parents.
5. Adult education provides the key to constructive relationships between the generations.

Teacher training

The role of the teacher must undergo fundamental change in any system of lifelong education. His function as conveyor of knowledge will diminish in importance and volume, all the more as he will be able to remit this task, to a large extent, to the technological media. On the other hand his role as educator will be strengthened. It should soon be recognised as inconceivable that a subject as precious as a child, with all the complexities of his characteristics and hopes, should be handed over to the mercies of an individual — the teacher — who is not in possession of the competence required for this delicate task. A child is not solely a number on a list, a good or a bad pupil, or less gifted for arithmetic or grammar; he is above all a human being endowed with personality. He has his own psyche, his sociological significance, his place in a series of contexts, his urges and his inhibitions; some roads are open to him and others closed. Is it conceivable that an adult holding so much power over a child should not be equipped to perceive that child, to understand his co-ordinates, to guide rather than judge, to draw advantage from every individual resource rather than punish every deficiency? All this presupposes a thorough theoretical and practical preparation including general psychology and the study of intelligence, as well as sociology in the broad sense of society in the mass and in the narrow sense of group sociology. What is needed here is an irreducible minimum of training which should be introduced forthwith in the preparation of teachers for their task, so as to eliminate wastage and build the foundations of lifelong education.

A COLLECTIVE ENTERPRISE

Research

If it is true that every life is a perpetual struggle, is it better to start preparing the future adult from school onwards for the coming contests, or on the contrary, at each successive stage and in the various types of training, to stress co-operation and intercommunication? Is it possible to create a state of equilibrium as between these conflicting demands of personality and of fate, and if so, how and through what channels?

This is one of the fundamental questions which every educator must face, whether he is concerned with curricula or with actual teaching, for upon the answer will to a large extent depend the general direction of instruction. But many other questions arise with equal sharpness:

What is the true equilibrium between individual and collective aims, and in particular how should the training needs of the individual, with all his capacities and hopes, be reconciled with the needs of selection?

How can we equate the demand for personalisation of teaching (taking into account all the individual traits of which the importance has been stressed throughout this study) with the universal features of human nature and its need for intercommunication?

What weight should be given to the different contents of curricula once we have rejected encyclopaedic teaching and placed the accent on method? What are the points of reference common to science, literature, philosophy and history that are essential to the development of the personality in its own social, political and historical context?

What balance should be sought between the acquiring of the needed disciplines, respect for the external establishment and the free

85

expression of the personality?

Within a particular training, what proportions should be established between games and study?

Are there optimum periods for apprenticeship, generally or in respect of certain particular disciplines such as languages, mathematics, instrumental skill, etc.?

What laws govern the development of the personality and the stages of growth of intelligence, sensitiveness, sociability, and so forth?

What are the values that underlie each type of instruction and training?

In the educational process, what shares should be allotted to school teaching, to out-of-school activities, to so-called 'parallel' schools, to the family, to the workshop, etc.?

To what extent and in what manner should education concern itself with prospects connected with manpower needs?

What attention should be paid to problems of employment opportunities?

Educators know some of the answers, or at any rate find themselves the interpreters of the answers supplied, explicitly or implicitly, by each of the educational systems now in effect. Every educator, whether he is conscious of it or not, has his own system of values and of points of reference. But what are the foundations of these doctrines, official or personal?

In most cases the corpus of solutions has no other bases than traditions, customs, an inheritance of thoughts and processes and a purely empirical acquaintance with the problems of education. These are no doubt valuable elements, and the value of practical experience, together with the thinking of the craftsmen of teaching upon their own activity, are irreplaceable. Nevertheless the magnitude of the problems involved, the complexity of the factors at work, the necessity to adapt or to conceive new solutions, all call today for more solid foundations than the subjective opinions or experience of individuals can provide. Having taken every precaution as to methods, having brought every needed correction to the urge for system, we cannot, if we wish to build lifelong education on sound bases, elude the necessity of travelling beyond the realm of opinions, and of building a science.

86

To the varied experience of the teachers must be added the incontrovertible evidence of the human sciences. In defining its objectives, programmes and methods, education cannot dispense with the vital contributions of psychology and sociology. Only the psychologist and professional analyst of character can throw light, for the educator's benefit, on the circumstances and timing of the developments of personality. Only they can provide the needed data regarding the psychical forces at work, the mental blocks, the difficulties of adaptation, etc.

Sociologists and political scientists will for their part highlight the role of education in the evolution of society, both as a product and as a factor. Who will calculate exactly the return to be expected from educational action, viewed both *per se* and in its relations with other forms of investment? The experience of artists, poets, composers, of men of science and of all who have found their vocation in the act of creation, will also have to be fully drawn upon, for they can furnish the most valuable evidence concerning the relationship between the construction of a work, of whatever nature, and the development of the personality.

If the desired new order is to take shape and become a reality it will be necessary to mobilise every resource, intellectual, emotional and practical, and all the forces that sustain the social edifice as a whole.

Experience gained in factories, fields and offices will prove as decisive in drawing up a new educational doctrine as the wisdom of philosophers, the inspiration of poets, and the constructions of scientists, both theoretical and practical.

If the soundness of these reflections is admitted, it becomes less and less thinkable that discussions on education, involving so many aspects of personality and affecting so many elements of the social fabric, can henceforward be left solely to the professionals of education. This is a collective enterprise, and all the circles involved must be associated not only with the work of research, but with the decisions.

The educational function

There will doubtless always be, in any given society, individuals, men and women, whose vocation is teaching. Education will continue to lead the way to professions, and the latter to call for specialised training. To provide a child's education, to carry through a training course, the teacher must master a number of techniques and possess the necessary qualifications. Teachers, moreover, in addition to their roles as instructors and trainers, render society the signal service of taking charge of children and adolescents while their parents carry out their duties, either professional or domestic.

Nevertheless the transformations which have taken place in educational thought and practice, together with their likely evolution, cannot fail to have repercussions on the function of the educator.

In admitting the notion that education reaches far beyond the limits traditionally assigned to it — in particular those of teaching — we must also accept that any person who, at a given moment and in given circumstances, has responsibilities for instruction and training, is an educator. This is clearly the position of the teacher, but it is also that of the physician, the priest, the foreman, the engineer, the agricultural demonstrator and the man responsible for a political, trade-union or co-operative structure. Parents are educators by priority and will increasingly remain so, and among others who hold this kind of responsibility, even if they are not always conscious of the fact, we must clearly include the managers and prime movers of the mass information media who, through radio, press, television and the screen, contribute powerfully to the making and moulding of minds, hearts and tastes.

All these categories and figures of modern societies constitute a great army of educators and swell the training resources available to these societies. But this does not mean that they are automatically qualified to exercise their responsibilities in an adequate manner. There are countless ignorant and clumsy parents who retard their children's development. There are many physicians who regard a sick person as a medical case rather than as an individual who requires advice and guidance. There are numerous programme directors who adopt the lowest denominator within their public, which they flatter by appealing to its passions and self-interest and by following the paths of facility.

The marshalling and mobilisation of these many resources in the interests of the educational development of individuals and societies accordingly raise problems both of conscience and of competence — the word 'conscience' being here taken in its double significance as both intellectual acceptance or awareness of a state of fact, the educational process, and as moral acceptance or acknowledgement of responsibility with all the consequences implied in different forms of action. But competence is also a necessity: there must be a clear view of the objectives to be reached, of ways of conveying messages, of what is good and what is bad, useful or harmful to men's natures. Should we not deduce from all this that an aptitude to educate should henceforward form part of the training of every individual, if only because every individual, as a general rule, will become a domestic partner and will have children to bring up? More specifically, it would seem clear that educational theory and practice have now become an integral part of the training of any individual belonging to a modern society whose occupation endows him with influence, authority or responsibility towards others.

Within the ambit of this collective enterprise it is highly desirable that all these participants in educational action, whether professional teachers or others, should remain in permanent communication and consultation, guiding one another and benefiting from each other's specific experience and contributions. Only on such terms can the structures of an authentic and vigorous form of lifelong education progressively take shape.

Towards an educational society

The logic of the development of lifelong education presupposes a transformation of the structures of society in a direction favourable to the growth of the personality. This fundamental aspect of the problem has already been touched upon in various parts of this study, in particular in the chapter dealing with the strategy of lifelong education. But at this point, when the collective character of the enterprise is being highlighted, together with the necessary alliances, we cannot lay sufficient stress on the predominant role of the politician and the administrator. The introduction of lifelong education is an essentially political undertaking, to the extent that the totality of the structures of the *polis* are involved in its realisation.

CONCLUSIONS

Lifelong education is still at the conceptual stage. As with other principles such as freedom, justice and equality, it will doubtless retain indefinitely that certain distance in relation to concrete achievements which is in the nature of concepts. If, however, the distance is too great, as is frequently the case for the other concepts just listed, scepticism will be aroused. The accusations of vagueness, formlessness and imprecision which are often aimed at this concept are not devoid of reason. If a notion is to emerge from limbo and to appear in its true light, it is essential that it should be reflected in facts and actions from which it can draw strength. For as long as analyses of lifelong education are not backed by a series of references to situations, structures, programmes, in brief, to all that is so aptly called the 'concrete', so long will it be difficult to win mass support for theses of which the foundations have so far been largely theoretical.

There is no gainsaying that lifelong education does not yet exist anywhere in the fullness of its aims. Certain forces are undoubtedly at work, and the world has not waited for theorists to express their views, or for committees to make recommendations, before entering upon the course of a form of education adapted to the becoming of things and beings. The elements with the aid of which the conceptual framework of the new education is taking shape are found in the solutions that individuals and groups apply, day by day and year by year, to new situations. Lifelong education has become not only desirable but possible only because new avenues have opened up. If, for example, we did not have the benefit of the appreciable contribution made by adult education, and more generally by out-of-school methods of training, if countries had not built up extensive networks of communication through radio and television, and if the means of universal instruction were not at hand, then our thoughts concerning lifelong education would be without meaning and would doubtless not even have begun to

91

take shape. Today, on the contrary, the enterprise lies in the realm of the possible, and lifelong education represents from now onwards a great hope. That hope rests upon faith in man and in his ability to become an adult responsible for his thinking, his feelings and his options — granted always that his creative powers have not been whittled away from the outset, either by a hostile world or by modes of training which pay no respect to man's originality and thrust.

PART II
DEMONSTRATIONS AND ILLUSTRATIONS

AIMS LINKED WITH LIFELONG EDUCATION

Man as he really is

The true subject of education is man in all his aspects, in the diversity of his situations and in the breadth of his responsibilities, in short, man as he really is.

Modern man is the victim of abstraction. Everything conspires to divide him and break his unity, e.g. the division of society into classes; fragmented work in which the individual can perceive neither the structures nor the overall goal of production and cannot manage to define his place in it; the contrast between manual and intellectual work and the two types of people this breeds; the conflict of ideologies and the crumbling of collective myths; and the dichotomy between body and mind and between material and spiritual values.

Man is lost amidst a multitude of images of himself and a multitude of incoherent and contradictory situations, trends and definitions. Education as it is planned and as it actually functions, particularly in the form of teaching, contributes greatly to this dissociation of the parts of the personality. One aspect of the person has been arbitrarily isolated for the needs of instruction, i.e. the intellectual aspect in its cognitive form, and the other aspects have been forgotten or neglected and either shrink to an embryonic state or develop in a disordered fashion and threaten the balance of the personality.

To meet examination needs, a further stage has been added to the initial abstraction. This stage does not accept the intellect as it really is, with its originality and its own powers but compares its performance with that of others in a continuous process of awarding marks. There is a massive substitution of the quantitative for the qualitative. The child becomes the subject of assessments and hence his development is arrested and fixed by a limited and arbitrary vision.

The competition established in this environment from earliest childhood also helps to narrow the field of human experience. The exchange, dialogue, communication and mutual enrichment which are indispensable to every man if he is to fulfil himself are reduced to their simplest expression.

The extension of educational experience, even to the detriment of other forms of experience, such as work, games or sentimental communication, keeps a young person in an artificial situation at a time when he is already in possession of his powers of feeling and acting. Under these conditions, it is not surprising that incurable traumatisms often result, and it is found that an adolescent educated in this way frequently has great difficulty in coming to terms with the world and establishing correct and constructive relationships with other people. Some essential parts of his being are either atrophied or temporarily paralysed to such an extent that he is scarcely civilised.

It is in order to fight against such a system and to remedy the destructive effects of modern civilisation that the foundations of a new education are being laid. The target is man as he really is and his actual dimensions. The characteristics of such a man may be seen as a series of pairs of determinations, some of which are complementary and others contradictory.

The aim of education is to cater for every aspect and dimension of the individual as a physical, intellectual, emotional, sexual, social and spiritual being. None of these components can or ought to be isolated and each in turn supports the others.

This individual is considered in two contexts: as an independent individual and in relationship with others and with society in general. He is at once isolated and involved.

He is a man given to responsibility, participation and exchange and not to passivity and competition.

He belongs alike to the particular and to the universal – to the particular in so far as he feels himself to be a member of society, acting as such and sharing the feelings, traditions and ways of life of a community, class or country; and to the universal in so far as he is able to perceive the common feature of mankind in the infinite diversity of human expression, has a sense of fellowship with other men, races and peoples and acquires a world outlook.

He is both a specialist, and skilled in a number of fields, but he uses his specialist knowledge to increase his understanding of other spheres of thought and activity.

He remains resolutely attached to his own state of immaturity and refuses to accept ready-made patterns of adult life.

He also rejects the various forms of rigidity and is for continual change and renewal.

He becomes, more and more, the subject of his own education.

He establishes a constructive and living relationship with time, which he regards not as an enemy but as an ally, and with his own lifespan.

He is the incarnation of life and movement and not of stability, stagnation and nostalgia.

Adaptability

The mind perceives change only when it is swift, a fact that everyone can verify when watching a film showing plant growth. Whereas in normal experience transformations are not perceptible, in the film — through the artificial shortening of the growth stages — the development of the plant is seen as if it were the body of an animal in motion.

This is precisely the way in which historians work. They eliminate an infinite number of details and circumstances and knit together moments which, in fact, are separated by what are sometimes considerable temporal distances. This is how they present the course of a life-history, the events of a day and the advent of a monarchy, and how they retrace the evolution of a civilisation.

In the existence of the great mass of human beings, changes were, for a long time, barely perceptible and difficult to grasp. They were too slow. An individual's journey through life proceeded, by and large, in the physical, intellectual and spiritual surroundings of his childhood and it required a crisis of major intensity and magnitude, such as a war or revolution, to project the human being into a different universe to which he must either adapt himself or run the risk of either disappearing or experiencing anguish and becoming unbalanced.

This latter situation, which has been the exception over the centuries, is now becoming the rule for a large proportion of mankind. The volume of changes occurring within the space of a generation and the gathering momentum of transformations in the world have been described on many occasions. There is a whole literature on the subject. It is now well established that from decade to decade, and sometimes even from year to year, individuals in an increasing number of societies are faced with changes of great magnitude affecting the various sectors of their life and involving the different aspects of their personality. In many disciplines, particularly in the sciences, knowledge hardly ever reaches a stable state. We see a growing flood of discoveries and new theories whose effect is to relegate the most firmly entrenched notions to the past. Relationships between the generations, between children and parents, between men and women, are also in a continuous state of upheaval. The very notion of 'adult' is called in question today. The same applies to the place and role of authority and the traditional dominant-dominated relationship. Customs, ideas and ideologies ebb and flow incessantly. One of the factors which used to make for stability of conditions and ways of life — one's profession — is subject to constant fluctuations. Technological progress and changes are such that countless workers are now experiencing the need for re-training and must even expect to change their profession several times during their working life. The result is that change is now not only perceived by everyone in its practical implications, but is regarded as one of the basic experiences of the majority of human beings.

There are many reasons why men are repelled by this movement that draws us inexorably in its wake. They are for the most part of an affective kind. For we have to break with our habits. People naturally cling to what they know and are associated with. They are reassured by familiar surroundings and experience of change often brings distress, regret or nostalgia. On the intellectual plane, they tend to see the relative and transitory as absolute and permanent, in terms both of knowledge and of belief.

This being so, it is not surprising that a growing number of people live today in a state of anguish. From the days of their childhood, family life and school, they have been accustomed to finding security and stability in the acquistion of knowledge firmly established in tradition and supported by the authority of their parents and of their intellectual and spiritual teachers. The future did not seem threatening

98

in so far as it was basically foreshadowed by the experience of their elders and the paths of their progress were traced for them in advance. Suddenly they have found themselves in an alien, unfriendly world in which they do not recognise themselves.

If modern man is to find release from his anguish and the future is to lose its threatening aspect for him, there must be radical transformations and changes in minds and attitudes with regard to life. A new conception of time must be created. Instead of regarding time as a negative factor, as man's enemy, always militating against him, it should be viewed as something positive, bringing human experience discoveries and progress. On this does love of life, *amor fati*, depend; and it naturally implies acceptance of risk and taste for adventure of all kinds.

Education is all-powerful in fostering this state of mind and attitude. It is the role of education to guide man's thoughts towards the past or towards the future, towards a state of rigidity or flux, towards the discovery of true security by becoming part of the movement.

There is no better general preparation for this readiness to accept innovation than the development of the scientific approach which, as we have said, is one of the basic components of modern humanism. Science is perception of the world, of a world subject to forces which sweep it along in a continual upheaval of structures and forms.

Development of creativity works along the same lines. There can be no creative activity by an individual or by a society unless obsolescence and renewal are accepted and welcomed as experience of life in action.

However, education for active acceptance of change includes an additional, specific element which is the historical approach. The new prominence given to the place and role of time in the various sectors of human thought and activity is one of the basic signs of progress of the modern mind and this is how it differs fundamentally from the classical attitude which inclines towards sameness and permanence. Historical thought has developed over the past century and a half to the extent that all knowledge, whether in the sphere of biology, art, ideas, or even of mental mechanisms, is now placed within the context of a given length of time. But this approach has not, up to now, found its way into education.

Time, as curricula are arranged at present, is considered only in the form of a specific subject dealing with the succession of periods in the life of peoples, and particularly of the privileged nation to which the pupils belong. Often the thread is missing — that of civilisation, which takes the work of men into account just as much as the action of succeeding dynasties and military conquests. It seems vital, however, in ensuring preparation for change, that all instruction should be given within the historical perspective. Whether this concerns science, literature, art or the various language disciplines, each of these individual themes cannot assume its true significance or make its full educational impact unless it is presented and explained within the context of its development and through the various phases of its evolution. It is the mind in action — at once destructive and creative — that has to be illustrated and made intelligible in all the breadth and diversity of its manifestations.

Adaptability to change is conceivable only in and through the most general education possible. It is the fate of modern man to have to face constant manifold innovations. This applies to the intellectual, spiritual and affective aspects of his world, as it does to the professional aspects. This being so, we are obviously doing him a disservice in providing him prematurely with too specialised a training.

Such training, limited in its aims, may well hinder modern man's acquisition of a true and broad understanding of this shifting world and his integration in the political, social and professional frameworks in which he is to develop. What is important, then, in order to provide him with the necessary flexibility and versatility, is not to make him absorb ready-made knowledge but to equip him intellectually and spiritually for research and discovery. Adaptability is thus closely linked with the aims of scientific reasoning, creativity and social commitment which make up the essential substratum for the well-balanced development of every personality.

Education for happiness

Is the aim of education to make men happy? It is not, if we consider happiness as an intrinsic reality, as something outside ourselves which

100

we may obtain or miss; it is, if we visualise happiness as a mode of being. There is a happy and an unhappy way of feeling settled in the world, of perceiving it, of establishing one's relationship with time and of communicating with other people.

Education does not enter into the picture if happiness or unhappiness is made to depend on the possession or lack of an object, whether it be a material asset such as a car, a toy, wealth, etc., or a moral asset such as possession of someone loved or public esteem. Education is powerless in this case, not only because it has no part to play in such ambitions, but also because this approach to happiness, as everyone knows by experience, in the end proves ineffective and meaningless. Education does come into the picture, however, if happiness is given its true meaning as a mode of being and a way of living one's life. Not only is a link between happiness and education then established but one might almost say that there is no true, firmly rooted and abiding happiness save that derived from the educational process. To quote Spinoza: 'Joy is man's transition from a lesser to a greater state of perfection; sorrow is man's transition from a greater to a lesser state of perfection.' If we translate joy by happiness we have the answer: happiness is linked with the exercise and feeling of power. Let us be quite clear — by power is meant true power, not the deceptive, alienating and dangerous power of controlling other people, but the power which really deserves the name, that of self-control. This kind of happiness is accessible to any man and is within everyone's reach, if certain conditions are fulfilled. Everyone is capable of effort, that moment in a man's existence which shows that he is 'in control'. Everyone is capable of making this effort to control himself on the countless occasions when lucidity must triumph over illusion, knowledge over ignorance, hope over despair and discouragement, confidence in others over mistrust and suspicion, love and understanding over hatred and misanthropy, and availability and transparency over refusal and opacity. These are the elements and moments of 'happiness', like those when a man states his own feelings in opposition to the sheep-like herd, counters ready-made conceptions with his personal and original view of the world, and prefers the judgement which he has formed on the basis of knowledge or reflection to vague, fluctuating opinions.

101

Reaching this state of power is not just a natural process. Left to himself, and if he be lucky, a man may well arrive at a state of vegetative beatitude which, for many, passes for happiness and even assumes some of its forms. Without mentioning the superficiality and vanity of what are known as 'pleasures', is it not nonetheless obvious that this self-possession on which a 'happy' lot depends, can be acquired only by work? Work means study, discipline and the discovery and use of the gifts and abilities enabling us to understand and communicate with others, and to find answers to the questions with which life, the world and the vicissitudes of the heart and mind are constantly facing us, even when we keep them on the confines of our consciousness. The pursuit of happiness then converges with the aims of education, and the paths leading to a happy existence are those followed during different phases of the educational process.

In other words, happiness and education are buildings. But unlike structures of wood and stone fixed in their relative immutability, these are buildings made of flesh and mind, expressions and instruments of life, and, like life, malleable and changing. The work of building up a happy existence through education has neither limit nor end. It is a long preparation and, as the well-known examples of artists and scholars clearly show us, it is only through a series of stages, of withdrawals and advances, of successes and failures seen in perspective and judged, and of relative or final victories, that a man attains to the full originality of his point of view and to freshness of outlook and feeling. Furthermore, each part of this construction itself has to be invented and imagined. An idea does not exist like an object, nor does a feeling or a relationship. If the idea, feeling or relationship is not built up and established as a triumph over doubt, a victory over hesitation or a winning battle against obscurity, not to say the affirmation of strength over weakness, it cannot exist and vanishes like a cloud. This intimate bond which lifelong education maintains with the substance of a human being and with his development is more compelling than the historical, sociological and economic reasons which make lifelong education a necessity. A state of this kind has nothing idyllic about it. It is a situation in which there is a place for tragedy. No one can hope to know happiness in his life unless he resigns himself to being constantly challenged, unless he is ready to meet with changes, separations and disappearances and unless he faces up resolutely to the unavoidable need to die unto himself several times in the course of his life. Whereas the patterns of family and school education have hitherto led to the construction of an untrue, frail and fixed image of happiness resting on an illusion of security, the aim of education is to teach individuals resolutely to accept risk, alteration and insecurity and to ally themselves with time, the destroyer of all things.

This individual, with a calling and capacity for happiness, is not the isolated individual of our atomised (in both senses of the word) societies but is linked to others, in communication with the structures and forces of a just society. This means that in our societies, which are based on inequality and, in thousands of ways, hinder communion and communication, the building of a 'happy' life as suggested here encounters many difficulties and obstacles. It is therefore perhaps not exaggeration to say that one of the fundamental justifications for the struggles being carried on throughout the world for equality, liberty and fraternity is that their aim is to create political and legal situations, in which everyone, for his own sake and for that of others, may be able to carry on this educational venture which is the essence and the expression of a happy life.

Education for the improvement of the quality of life

The aims of education also come face to face with the components of what is today called the quality of life. This is a vague idea indeed. What is there which does not enter into the quality of life? What helps to make life a reality full of virtues or charms, worthy to be lived with enthusiasm and pleasure or, on the contrary, makes it a scowling monster imposing its presence and domination through the powers of routine and resignation? Everything comes into play, the air we breathe, be it pure or contaminated, the water we drink, be it healthy or polluted, and the landscape around us, be it pleasant or dismal; a hostile environment which causes distress or a friendly environment where a man feels supported, encouraged and loved. Do working conditions, transport and housing come into the quality of life? Yes, of

103

course they do if we hold to a broad and all-embracing view of the qualitative aspect of life. No, they do not, will say others who fear that this notion will result in all the inhabitants of the earth being lumped together, equally victims of physical and moral corruption, whether they be rick or poor, black, yellow or white. For upholders of this view, and particularly for political and trade union militants, it is a concept which is either ineffectual or dangerous, in so far as it is liable to make differences of status and position be forgotten and discourage the mass of ordinary people from carrying on the fight for their class interests as well as for their pay claims and for equality of opportunity.

It is nevertheless true that we have to face the problems of the environment, pollution, etc., that no political consideration can detach us from them, and that education plays an important, not to say conclusive rôle among those factors which influence the quality of life. First of all, education may be destructive in character. It may be a source of disturbance and a kill-joy. Many men and women who are ill at ease in this world and suffer from psychological or emotional traumatisms, who do not manage to establish satisfactory relationships with other people on the basis of equality and exchange and who have an unhappy and misanthropic outlook, impose it on those around them and use it as an instrument of moral torture, owe their unhappiness in life to the education which they received. A disunited or overbearing family and dictatorial, unimaginative school are examples of destructive environments and harmful things which require to be changed radically.

On the other hand, everything which has been said elsewhere in this work on the aims of education in relation to individual and collective aims in life applies to the qualitative objectives of education. To take but one example, the fight against noise is not only a question of legislation and administrative decrees. If a person on a moped is not to wake up 500,000 town-dwellers in the middle of the night by making his machine backfire, he must be brought up to respect other people, to take their feelings into consideration and to follow the principles and rules of democratic life. The same applies to those who force the noise of their transistor radios or the din of their television sets on others, finding in this, moreover, a cure for and a drug to help them

104

fight the ravages of a boredom whose source is to be found in the manifold physical, intellectual, moral and aesthetic 'illiteracies' from which they suffer.

However important the place of education in this field, its limits must be perceived. If the fish we eat is impregnated with mercury, if radioactive dust floats in the air, if the rivers are lifeless and if the forest trees are felled, it is not because the polluters are ignorant of the consequences of what they are doing or even that they are insensitive; it is because the law of economic interests or the requirements of power politics have overridden all other considerations.

Education for peace and international understanding

If it be true that peace is society's greatest good, that the very survival of the human species is threatened by conflicts which are liable to make whole regions of the earth, if not the entire globe uninhabitable, we are naturally led to ask how far it is the aim of education to prepare men to reject war and seek peace. This is undoubtedly one of the most difficult and delicate questions to answer. If education can contribute to the relaxing of tension between peoples, we can but conclude that to make individuals peace-loving is the primary purpose of every form of education.

However, such a proposition runs counter to the theory of war. Is war really born in the minds of men, as an illustrious statesman and philosopher proclaimed just after the Second World War?

It does not seem to be quite so simple. If we say 'in the minds of men', we have to specify which men. Certainly not in the minds of the fighting men in a national war, who have usually never met the individuals at whom they take aim and have no feelings about them other than those inspired by political pressures and the unleashing of group passions. Men who today are enemies to be hated and destroyed will be regarded as friends or brothers tomorrow if the wind turns and the colour of their flag changes. If education comes in at this stage, it does not avert conflict unless it stirs people to disobedience and revolt. All it can do is to banish base or futile feelings — to kill or wound a man is no reason for hating, despising or humiliating him.

105

So it is at the level of the decision-makers that mental attitudes can come into the picture. When a council of ministers decides to negotiate and to keep on negotiating rather than use force, why does it do so? The main consideration is assuredly the respective strength of the opposing parties. What are our chances? How many divisions can we muster? What are our stocks of munitions? Can we rely on our allies? Education is not alien to the development of such reasoning. It helps the leaders to make correct and precise calculations and not to deceive themselves regarding objectives and means and the relationship between them. It helps also to inspire in them those human feelings and humanitarian considerations, which are never completely lacking in people of this kind.

This brings us to a general problem of civilisation, of which observance of the law of nations, to take only this essential aspect, is a part. It is a well known fact, for example, that in eighteenth-century Europe, conflicts between monarchs were waged in a legalistic atmosphere reflecting the ethics of Enlightenment, which precluded the idea of exterminating the enemy — an idea which was enthusiastically taken up by the national and social entities which emerged from the revolutions of the nineteenth and twentieth centuries. From the standpoint of war and peace, this may be regarded as a regression, a return to the barbarities and fanaticism of earlier times, even if, in other respects, a more optimistic view may be taken.

The way in which conflicts between peoples are triggered off, how they are carried on and how they are settled therefore depend quite clearly on the general level of ethics, on the nature of ideas and mental attitudes. Here education comes into its own. It does so indirectly, although its influence is very powerful.

At this level, warlike feelings are rooted in aggressiveness, the negation of others and lack of imagination. Everything in education which helps individuals to live at peace with themselves, to be what they claim to be, to come to terms with the diverse aspects of their personalities, to fit into the processes of exchange and participation, and to escape from the unhappiness of isolation and solitude, has a pacifying effect. Hostility to others, the desire and the will to destroy, are closely related to frustration, individual and social failure, resentment and various inferiority complexes. In the exaltation of national sentiment persons suffering from a feeling of inferiority find an opportunity of boosting their self-esteem at little cost, especially as they can rest on the support of their fellow citizens and have a clear conscience in the knowledge of their rightness and superiority over foreigners.

Inculcating a spirit of peace in individuals is therefore bound up with all the other ultimate ends of education, whether intellectual, affective or social. If this spirit does not exist at all times and at all stages of education, it is like a tree without roots and it will not withstand the slightest gust of wind. Special importance, however, should be attached to the development of a democratic spirit and its international aspects. In the complicated, intricate game of politics and diplomacy, the attitudes of mind of the peoples concerned cannot fail to carry weight and wield influence. When the authorities have to do with majorities of 'adult' citizens or active minorities, they cannot use those they govern for their belligerent purposes with the same ease as when they are dealing with a malleable, ill-informed people, who are misled concerning their real interests. It even happens that realisation of the injustice and absurdity of a policy changes the course of events and imposes peace — generally at the cost of a revolution.

It might be mentioned that educational activities directed towards development are also of overriding importance, if it is true that disparities in incomes and living conditions engender tensions which in themselves imperil peace.

Does this mean that peace should not be taught as a separate subject? In the light of what has been said above as to the indivisibility of the spirit of peace, it would seem that the psychological and moral causes of aggressiveness towards foreigners should be fought in the context of each subject. There is a way of teaching history, geography and philosophy which fosters a belligerent attitude inasmuch as it blocks understanding. Everything which helps us to see foreigners not as an abstract entity, the enemy, but as a multitude of self-determining human beings with their joys and sorrows and their problems, everything which enables us to discern what is common to mankind in the various forms of expression, is conducive to the arousing of peaceful inclinations. When this view is taken, the concern for truth and knowledge coincides with the most patent and real interests of a civilisation beneficial to mankind.

CONTENT AND METHODS

Until recently, the educator possessed a singularly limited number of methodological tools – oral exposition, repetition, exercises, lessons, with, as powerful adjuncts, punishment and reward. Limited though it was, this stock-in-trade suffices in so far as the result sought was the transmission of knowledge which was itself limited in nature and in composition and did not entail overstepping the boundaries of a school or university curriculum. Methods rested on a set of assumptions and comparatively arbitrary choices, some deliberate and some not. The first assumption was the all-powerfulness of words (particularly the teacher's words) when it came to moulding the mind and enriching the fund of knowledge of the school pupil, the student or anyone else in process of learning. The second assumption was that all minds subjected to the influence of education were substantially alike, that reason was the same everywhere and in everyone, the only difference being one of degree: some are more gifted than others; some are keen on their work, others are lackadaisical or refractory.

The system was based, too, on acceptance of failure. If, despite the teacher's efforts and the alternation of punishment and reward, some lagged behind and did not manage – or only partly managed – to assimilate the substance of what was taught, they were automatically classed as bad pupils, not gifted, lazy or unconscientious.

Our age is witnessing a profound change in this conception of education whether in the narrow or in the broader sense. In the content-method relationship, which is central to educational theory and practice, the emphasis, which used to be placed on content, is gradually shifting towards method. There are many reasons for this, and they are becoming powerful enough to overcome the resistance and inertia which are particularly rife in educational circles.

With regard to method, the first factor in innovation was the progress of educational thought from within. Despite the impermeability of teaching practice, turned in on itself for centuries, it was impossible for the conquests of psychology and sociology to remain completely external to it. The studies of Freud, Piaget and their faithful — or not so faithful — disciples, the research carried out by Dewey or Rogers and their followers in the United States and that carried out by Pavlov's school finally exerted an influence on the processes employed in education and the concepts governing it. Unless an educator is particularly resistant to information or hostile to change, he can no longer ignore the complexity of human beings or the factors involved in the development of the personality; some of these are intellectual but the majority have their origins and their basis in biology, the emotions and social instincts. The diversity of natures, temperaments and vocations has been brought fully to light, in particular as a result of the work done by the various schools of characterology. The moral attitude is also losing ground as understanding grows.

Here we can also see the effect of an advance made by civilisation, which is, incidentally, somewhat paradoxical. While regression is to be observed throughout the world in regard to the respect due to an adult, to his rights and his person, at the same time the child has become the subject of increased consideration. This is in striking contrast with the morality and ideas prevalent only a century ago, as borne out by documents, stories and chronicles. Children are tending to be regarded as precious beings who cannot be treated lightly and whom we must avoid damaging psychologically. Nor is economic thought alien to the educational movement. The traditional system, perfectly adapted to singling out the gifted pupils has proved to be ruthlessly wasteful in terms of forces and energy.

In some countries at least, practical experience of out-of-school education, and particularly of adult education, has produced new ideas and relationships which have also penetrated education in general. It was in this branch of activities that the methods of group work were evolved and that the group leader gradually superseded the traditional teacher figure.

Finally the various movements which have occurred, first in university circles, then in secondary schools, the resistance, the revolts

110

and, generally speaking, the challenging of educational methods, have
done much to upset the traditional order.

A new methodological approach

Under these various influences and pressures the principles of a new
methodology of education are gradually being evolved:

From the curriculum to the learning situation

The first principle of this new educational creed is the importance
attached to the substratum of education – the group or the individual,
young or not so young – in a learning situation. In relation to the pupil
or the student, the curriculum tends to take on secondary, or in any
case relative, importance. No doubt there is still knowledge to convey
and skills to be acquired or rather mastered. But the essential aim of
any aspect of education, whether study, exercise or practice, is a
change in the human being as a whole. It is the human being who in
a sense becomes the content of his own education. It is this content,
this 'raw material' which, through education, takes shape and acquires
the skills and competence which were only virtual in the individual
before.

One consequence of this emphasis is that the principal agent of
education is no longer the master or mistress, the teacher, the
instructor. It is the individual in the process of education. It is he who
develops, it is he who transforms himself, it is he who actualises his
own potentiality by a process which is peculiar to him and for which
there is no substitute.

Self-education is therefore the main object of training.

Self-education has a pathetic history. It has produced more sorrow
than joy, more failures than successes. Until now the self-taught were
those members of the population who set out in quest of knowledge
and skills without having received the formal education by which those
more privileged had benefited. Deprived of references and the
traditional intellectual tools, they ventured away from the beaten
tracks, to explore some corner of the literary, philosophical and/or
scientific universe. The more gifted succeeded in their venture and

111

even made discoveries worthy of notice, but these were often paid for very dearly. Many did not find what they were seeking, either because they had reached blind alleys or because the magnitude and intensity of the effort required discouraged them. But it is a diametrically different form of self-education with which we are concerned here. It is now a question of equipping everyone, at school or university, wherever or whenever the educational process is involved, with the elements and tools which will enable him or her to continue the quest for knowledge throughout life and so always to move forward.

Motivation and functional nature

In the light of the foregoing, motivation, which is frequently referred to in writings or statements on education, assumes its full significance. In the old system, inner motivation was not essential. As a matter of fact, it was only present in a minority, made up of those who by temperament, heredity or social and cultural pressure were naturally disposed to make the kind of effort asked of them. For the majority, the impetus usually came from the person directing operations, the teacher. The system of marks, rewards and punishments, praise and reprimands, was there to sustain the wavering efforts of pupils. Only with the help of these traditional stimulants did they finally battle through to the end of their studies, culminating in an examination which declared them worthy or unworthy of crossing the threshold of the adult world. It was in the main a blind effort whose significance was not clearly apparent. After all, was it not the lot of childhood to be subject to external laws and to learn the uses of freedom and independence through protracted experience of subjection? It is not surprising under the circumstances that for most 'pupils' education remained superficial and deviant — and still is so where the traditional patterns are immutable. It is superficial in so far as the instruction received does not penetrate below the surface of the mind, all the rest being defended by the combined effects of indifference and resistance (active or passive according to the temperament). There is no other reason for the illiteracy of the masses, which is most manifest in the dislike of reading, even when books are readily available. This education is deviant in so far as it creates in individuals a distrust, sometimes even a profound

112

loathing, of anything resembling a cultural effort. In many minds, the two concepts of culture and school are inseparable and both are equally disliked.

So education — and within education, teaching — cannot evade the great law governing human activity, which is interest. If studies are to be interesting they must correspond to some desire. If learners are to be ready to make an effort and to employ all their energies, the aim must be clear and the result must be worth the effort.

A considerable number of factors are involved in arousing motivation or, conversely, in blocking it. Individualisation plays its part. What pleases and attracts one person does not suit another but puts him off. Of course there is a limit to the individual approach and no education is possible if there is too much dividing up. However, no educator can ignore or neglect the importance of personal inclinations and tastes, and of each one's individual pace. The two vital moments are at the beginning and the end of the different operations. In the beginning, it is the attention-winning phase, preparation for work; at the end, it is the clear view of the goal to be reached, bound up with the main aims of individual and social life: pleasure, play, wealth, prestige, fidelity, group constructing, etc. In this connexion two observations must be made.

(a) When it comes to individualising the educational process, this by no means entails a contradiction with group goals. On the contrary, an individual effort cannot fully succeed unless it is instigated and backed by the efforts of all, whether in a group or in a society. It is not by chance that the most powerful incentives to study obtain in periods of great social upheaval or the collective advance of a class or of a whole population.

(b) The functional side of education provides the strongest motives for study. That education cannot take place effectively in the vacuum of abstraction, pursuing ends peculiar to itself, but that it must be related to strong interests of everyday life, career, politics, improve-ment of living conditions of the community, has been observed and expressed in theoretical form by many educationists over the past fifty years. One of Unesco's programmes added fresh lustre to this principle. As everyone knows, on the basis of a critical analysis of

113

experiments previously carried out in many countries, Unesco recognised the decisive importance of the functional character of literacy training for the masses. In this particular case, the functional factor is economic and it is bound up with the improvement of production. However, it does not preclude other factors which strengthen and support the economic drive, such as nation building.

Group work

The old system rested entirely on competition. This is understandable for two fundamental reasons. In the absence of genuine, profound motivation resulting from the individual's real relation to learning, competition was a convenient means of securing the adhesion of the members of a group. And it is true that the desire to shine, to be the best and to win against the others is a powerful instinct in every individual. The second reason is inherent in the very nature of traditional education, in which the emphasis is laid on selection rather than on training. When the object is no longer to select the best but to provide equal opportunities for all, the methods cannot remain the same. The emphasis is now laid on the pooling of the resources, skills and knowledge of everyone with a view to the common pursuit of knowledge. Such is the spirit which inspires and governs experiments in group work. So far the sphere in which this approach to education has had a chance of being applied on the widest scale and with the greatest vigour is out-of-school education and adult education in particular. Elsewhere group work is practised only in sporadic and marginal fashion, so deeply and strongly rooted is the tradition of competition. But when adult education is not content with reproducing the system taken over from school and university education and frees itself from concern with examinations and rewards, it shows a preference for team work. Organised and controlled discussion is the natural form assumed by this educational process.

It is also this educational structure which has given rise to the new educator, regarded and acting as an organiser, who inspires and creates situations conducive to exchange and communication, rather than as a teacher properly speaking.

114

Creativity and non-directive methods

These two terms are not synonymous, but they are so often associated that it will be best to deal with the two concepts together.

The starting-point for considering creativity is to think about man's estate and his calling.

Is man made to follow, to obey, to carry out orders and to follow the trodden ways? Can he find satisfaction or fulfil his destiny in so doing? Or, on the contrary, does success in life lie in the assertion of the originality of each being, in the full and free expression of the poetic instinct? In the first instance, there is security, in the second, adventure. On the one hand, there is the search for protection, on the other, acceptance and love of risk, of all forms of risk, the risk of deceiving oneself and being deceived, the risk of discoveries, of being discovered, of experiencing the great joys of life – the joys of physical or intellectual conquests, or of conquests of the heart. For each of these two alternatives there is a price to pay. To be sure, the price of creativity is incomparably higher, since, to keep it up, all one's capacities and qualities must be engaged, whereas the price of security is the fairly modest one of discipline.

The two instincts – the instinct to seek security and the instinct to seek adventure – coexist in most people, although in different proportions according to temperament, age and sex. So encouraging one or the other is a question of choice. What can tilt the balance on the side of risk, its acceptance and the willingness of individuals to incur it is realisation of the simple fact that, for all mankind any security is false security. No such thing exists in nature. It is an artificial structure, frail and constantly called into question. Anyone who settles down into some sort of security, be it of money or of status, is potentially in danger and under a perpetual threat. The psychological lot of this type of person and of the kind of civilisation which develops according to this pattern is to be forever anxious and on the defensive. What is accepted as a general rule is seen to be even more patently true in this world of wars, revolutions, crises and declining values of all kinds.

The methods of traditional education were conceived entirely in terms of the first alternative, that of security. Furthermore, such a

115

choice is in line with the more or less explicit wishes of parents and what is expected by all types of authority, both temporal and spiritual. The smoothly constructed system of competitive examinations and awards by means of which everyone received his due in accordance with his merits and his conformity to the pattern, the division of learning into curricula, the marking, the *ex cathedra* lectures and the transmission of codified knowledge were all means of securing the foundations of an order resting on respect for hierarchies, the untroubled conscience of the winners and the resigned acceptance of the losers in the competition.

This is the order which is challenged by those who see in creativity the essence of the educational process. The notion of creation is indeed so broad and so complex that it is highly unlikely that everyone understands it in the same way and has the same conception of its content. This is a difficulty which must be accepted and faced. Nor can we overlook the necessity of dispelling certain illusions and much confusion. Creativity does not entail giving a free rein to every expression of human nature. The imitation of selected models is also a stage on the path to invention and discovery. Nor is there any question of denying the part played by discipline or of rejecting rules. However, the only discipline and rules which are consistent with invention in the long run are those which the individual works out for his own use. What stands out is that schooling, and education in general, as practised today, largely stifles and paralyses creative spontaneity. Under the influence of psychological and educational research with, in the forefront, that of Rogers and his team in the United States, a series of methods of training have been evolved, similar in conception, diverse in application. They are eloquently termed: non-directive methods. Their common feature is that they reduce to the minimum the direct intervention of the teacher, but without his role being diminished. The teacher's presence is essential to the establishment of the type of relations between members of a group which bring out psychic forces often buried in the unconscious, either by routine or by a combination of blocks and taboos.

It is too early to assess properly the results of this type of training, which is still in the experimental stage and has as yet scarcely spread

116

beyond certain adult education circles. However, the non-directive approach has already proved to be a most encouraging answer to some of those who are trying to know and assert themselves. It is to be foreseen that the spirit behind this research and some of the means employed will permeate all educational circles hostile to the sclerosis of the mind and the personality.

I might add that the teaching of science is also conducive to creativity – if the teacher does not confine himself to providing data and leading pupils along beaten tracks but opens their minds to the scientific method, that is, to the spirit of inquiry, investigation and verification, taking nothing for granted.

Methods and instruments

The criteria for selection

The preceding paragraphs describe a method which, in varying degrees, can serve as a basis for putting any modern education system into practice. The choice of means will largely depend on the fundamental policy alternatives chosen by those in charge of education and on the pressures exerted on them by the various categories of users. But there can only be alternatives where choice is possible, in other words where there are sufficient natural or, more particularly, financial means or resources to make possible the introduction and dissemination of those methods which, because of their nature and scope, have received the approval of experts.

Word and image

As regards educational methods, the scene is dominated at present by the stormy relationship between the two main vehicles of thought and feeling, word and image. Words can appear in many forms, either spoken in a lecture or radio broadcast or linked to other media as in television. Images too appear in very varied forms, from posters to documentary films.

The role of the image has always been to inform or to stimulate. In education, however, it took second place as long ago as the sixteenth century after the introduction and subsequently the domination of the

117

verbal message, principally in written form. *Doctus cum libro* was the formula of knowledge. The basic techniques of the mind's workings, especially rhetoric and logic (*logos*: word, reason) were bound up with the appropriate manipulation of words and syntactical connexions. The only possible approach to truth was thought to be the correct use of judgement and reasoning, the building blocks of which were words joined together in a coherent and systematic way. School and university teaching was based almost exclusively on communication of this kind. It is this supremacy which is now being challenged, in practice and in theory. Modern man acquires most of his information from sources other than written texts. Information and data about the physical and non-physical world come to him in the most varied ways through words (recorded or not) and, to an increasing extent, through images. Visual representation has invaded everybody's world wherever the modern way of life has reached.

Is this a good or a bad thing? The answer is largely subjective. It depends on one's conception of the conditions for acquiring knowledge, the nature of learning and the positive or negative effect of the traditional rules of the logical game. Those who support the claims of the image condemn the harm done by bookish, backward-looking civilisation, attached to traditional values and tending to confuse style with intellectual precision. They point to the superiority of a medium which appeals to the intuition and whose message has a direct meaning which can be deciphered without the long preparatory stages required by mastery of the written message.

On the other hand, there are those who pin their faith on the written medium alone. They are deeply distrustful of the visual message, seeing it as the symbol and, to a certain extent, the instrument of what they condemn and reject in the manifestations of the modern spirit and which can be summed up as the withering away of reflective thought. The image is the immediate present, the intrusion of sensation (not to say the sensational). They feel that people are dominated by posters, television, the cinema and the illustrated weekly and that under the all-powerful impact of these media on the imagination, the bulwarks and defences patiently constructed by centuries of written civilisation are crumbling.

118

There is some truth in both contentions. For a mind endeavouring to unravel the world's complexities and find its way through them, there are, it seems, as many dangers in the verbal, book-oriented approach as in the visual approach. Both give rise to illusions against which it is advisable and vital to forearm oneself. This, though, is not really the problem. Instead of setting one against the other, it is fairer and more productive to put these two broad categories of media side by side, to see what resources they offer for knowledge and education and, in the light of indispensable methodological criteria, to study how they can best be employed (timing, conditions of use, etc.) to render the services which may be expected of them.

In this connexion, there are two points to be considered:

(a) In most cases, the best solution, wherever possible, is to combine the different approaches, which complement each other and make up each other's deficiencies and defects: for instance, a television programme introducing an author and encouraging the reading of his books, or a book about a country where the pictures and text are used in counterpoint (and the pictures are not just the visual illustration of the text) and where the picture expresses what the text cannot adequately express and vice versa. Progressive forms of modern education provide remarkable examples of this kind of approach.

(b) A criticism made of any medium may prove groundless at a later stage in its development. This is true of television which was rightly criticised for its inability to fit in with a flexible timetable and the non-repetitive nature of its message. The recent invention of video-tape recording meets the dual requirement of flexibility in time and repetition of the message.

Innovation and tradition

It is thought in some educational circles that innovation in teaching methods as in any other aspect of education is good in itself, the argument being that new means are required to meet new situations, that by their nature and scope, traditional means are an obstacle to necessary progress, and that if the paths followed by education are the same ones as have been trodden over the centuries by generations of professional teachers, the substance of education cannot fail to be affected thereby.

119

Arguments of this kind carry a certain weight, of course, and it is impossible to deny the need to link substance and form in any effort at renewal. In the present case, however, novelty should neither receive automatic acceptance nor preclude the use of well-established methods. The only guide is whether the means are suitable to the end. What is most important, in any case, is the methodology, i.e. the general spirit and the lines of emphasis. This is the level at which invention and imagination, allied to rationalisation, are needed. In many cases, the instruments or the techniques selected are of themselves neutral and acquire their significance and force only through the spirit and the manner in which they are used.

Range and penetration

As long as education was only for a small élite, the range of the media was not a particularly important criterion. As soon as education emerged as a universal right and became available to the broad masses of the world's population, the relationship between the strictly educational value of the medium and its penetrating power had of necessity to be taken into consideration. *A priori*, a radio programme which can reach millions of people at once takes precedence from this point of view over a discussion by a group leader. Technical as well as economic considerations can swing the balance in favour of extensive education programmes employing the mass media. The criterion of range and power of penetration cannot be considered in isolation from the rest, any more than can any other criterion of selection. One always returns to the basic questions: Who is education aimed at in its general or specific aspects? What effects and results does one wish to obtain (e.g. rapid spread of superficial notions or a thorough training in the ability to study, think and form a judgement)? What stages does education follow (in the short, medium and long term) and what are the principal media used at each of these stages?

Examination of the means available

The means available must be examined in the light of the methodology set out above and using some of the criteria for selection which have been mentioned.

Taking education in all the true breadth and scope of the term, it is clear that there are innumerable ways of educating and training people of all ages, and that these cannot be rigidly classified. Moreover, if the professional educator is imbued with the principles of an education which draws upon all the sources of life and all the forms of experience, if he can see clearly what he is aiming at and knows how knoledge is acquired and how the personality develops, he will be capable, in order to achieve his aim, of taking advantage of all the opportunities and all the material and technical resources available to him. If necessary, he will invent new ones or find new uses for the old.

Despite this fluid situation, which is peculiar to education, the experience of educational institutions and educators has produced a number of relatively stable and solid forms which have proved their worth and cannot be ignored. There exists a stock of means, techniques, aids and instruments which, if properly known and used, offers resources which could not reasonably be disregarded.

Traditional methods

Lesson and lecture. These, for centuries, have been the most widely used methods of education. The paths of lifelong education, naturally, lead quite another way. There is, of course, still room in any kind of teaching for lectures, provided they are set in a much wider context, at the right time, and as part of a succession of educational operations. At certain intervals, which vary according to the subject and to the age of the students, it is valuable to present part of what is known or a particular portion of knowledge in a coherent exposition which opens up horizons for the mind and awakens a pupil's interest in finding out more for himself. In any given group of pupils or students, however, this kind of intellectual and artistic exercise should not be the preserve of a single person and it takes on a genuine educational significance only if each member of the group is called on to speak at some time or other. Furthermore, the lecture or lesson will cease to be central to education but will play an intermittent and subsidiary role and will become meaningful by virtue of the rational place alloted to them in the overall scheme of education.

121

Group techniques. The methodological principle of exchange and communication finds its commonest expression in education in the organisation of group work.

There have been countless studies and experiments over the last thirty years concerning the group, its functions, its functioning, its educational effects and the different ways in which it can be organised. It is obvious that putting individuals together is not enough to start an educational process going as if by magic. It has been found, in fact, that a wrongly composed and poorly organised group can have harmful effects. Blockages occur and a clumsy or premature use of certain group techniques can cause difficulty and may even be dangerous for the particularly sensitive individuals, the balance of whose personality can be disturbed almost to the point of loss of identity.

Such drawbacks are inherent in any method and it is important to be aware of them. Experience has, however, shown group work to be of irreplaceable value, particularly in non-formal education. In well-conducted group activity, the individual gains a heightened awareness of his identity *vis-à-vis* others and develops a fundamental part of his character, the relationship with others. The ever-present competition factor tends to become less important in the group and gives way to the factor of mutual enrichment through the interplay of differences.

For a group to function satisfactorily, it is vital not only for all its members to share a common spirit but also for a number of rules to be observed. The rules are the substance of a method which is worked out little by little on the basis of observation and interpretation of successes and failures, and they concern the number of participants, the arrangement of the premises, the placing of participants with respect to each other, procedure e.g., the rôle of the various members of the group, the function and rôle of the person in charge, the function and rôle of an observer, often chosen in turn from group members, the organisation, functioning and phasing of the different kinds of discussion, etc. Light is thrown on these various aspects by systematic research, known by the general name of group dynamics, which is coming to occupy an ever-increasing place and to have growing importance in the field of educational psychology.

The value and significance of group work naturally depend to a great extent on the intellectual and, more generally, cultural material the group has to work on. This shows the importance of preparatory work by the person or persons in charge. It is their task, for example, to provide documentation on the subject being studied. Similarly, group work goes hand-in-hand with the rational use of information supplied by the mass media.

However important this aspect of the methodology may be, there is one precaution which must be observed. One cannot expect everything of the group and entrust everything to it. Side by side with group work, there is individual work, which is just as important and as vital, if only because an individual, for much of his life, is alone and isolated and because such essential aspects of intellectual activity as the exercise of judgement can only be experienced in the solitude of the individual mind.

A SPECIAL CASE: FORMAL EDUCATION

When one considers the heavy burden which educational activities place on the finances and economy of every country, and when one looks at the amount of human effort which goes into teaching, one can hardly refrain from looking into education to see whether it is serving its purpose — i.e., whether it is responding adequately to all these challenges. Is it efficient? What is its cost benefit ratio? Does it help people to fulfil their human destiny? Is it successful as an equalising and democratising force? These are the questions which we shall examine in the following paragraphs.

Education and work

Most teachers acknowledge only grudgingly the close relationship between their activities and the needs of the economy. They see their functions, as a rule, in a different light: to instruct and train individuals on an abstract plane where institutions are of no account and where such links with production and administration as exist are purely accidental. For such 'utilitarian' purposes, there is technical education and, of course, the training of society's professional cadres (doctors, engineers, lawyers and teachers) at the higher education level. In fact, the links between the economic and educational worlds are not only close but also strong, and they work both ways: the country's economic activities supply educational establishments with the resources they need — starting with the money needed for school buildings and teachers' salaries; in turn, the health and balance of the economy depend on the kind of instruction and training which the various elements of the population receive.

In this connexion, a number of observations are called for:

(a) Except in the case of technical training (and some sectors of higher education), the future adult is not prepared by education to

124

cope with his real situation, which is essentially that he is destined to become a worker. Culture and work are considered separately, as if they belonged to different worlds. There is no continuity between the world of formal education and that of the everyday existence of most human beings; any communication between the two is merely fortuitous and intermittent.

(b) To the extent that education does aim to provide a vocational training, it operates very largely in a vacuum. In many instances, young people undergo vocational training without the educational authorities (and, above them, the political authorities) bothering to ascertain what the corresponding job openings are. In France, for example, it is reckoned that of every 100 students in the arts faculties, only six are sure to find, on reaching adulthood, a job in keeping with their capacities, a teaching post, for example. In some subjects, such as sociology or psychology, the situation is even more alarming. Meanwhile, industry is short of the engineers and technicians which it needs. In India, the number of higher education graduates who are trying vainly to find a use for their diplomas runs into hundreds of thousands, not only on the arts side but also in the scientific and technical disciplines. Quite apart from the personal ordeals and the obvious psychological suffering and shock which it causes, such a situation is both anomalous and dangerous: anomalous because it means an enormous wastage of a nation's resources and energy, and dangerous to the social equilibrium in that the victims do not accept their problems with resignation, but seek a solution in various forms of violence.

It is probably in the developing countries that this problem is at its most acute. The reasons are plain: in most cases, especially in Africa and Asia, the educational systems are a recent acquisition and their form and content are those inherited from the powers formerly administering those territories. The rift between the educational system and the people's material circumstances and way of life is even wider than in the former colonial countries where, however out of date the educational structures may be, they are at least a product of those countries' history, which is not the case in the Third World. Hence it is no surprise that, despite the spectacular progress which we noted

125

earlier, schools and universities in these countries succeed in training only a meagre proportion of the technical and administrative personnel which they need. The typical situation is under-administration on the one hand, and massive unemployment among graduates on the other.

The unsuitability of existing structures is glaringly apparent in rural areas, where the great majority of these countries' populations still lives. Occasional efforts have been made to give syllabuses a rural orientation, but usually these country-folk find that what they learn not only refers to geographically remote situations, but at the sociological, cultural and psychological level, relates almost exclusively to urban contexts. Here, too, the link between education and life is broken, resulting, among other things, in the impoverishment of cultural experience and a temptation to leave the rural areas. In fact, a short-term result of schooling, in a great many cases, is to encourage people to abandon the villages and swell the urban population. In these circumstances, some people understandably take the view that education, as it operates in many parts of the world, is an obstacle to development. A dissociation of work and economic matters in general from education also afflicts most of the programmes which aim to stamp out illiteracy among adults. For the most part, the intentions are praiseworthy: to meet the aspirations of the people, to redress an injustice, to prove how much importance governments attach to raising the cultural level of the people, etc., but results rarely come up to expectations. After the first flush of enthusiasm, interest in reading and writing fades. Motivation of a 'cultural' nature is not strong enough to stimulate a long-lasting commitment on the part of individuals and groups, for whom the problems of subsistence are a matter of urgency. Even when good results are obtained, they rest on shaky and unreliable foundations. Relapse into illiteracy is the rule in cases where literacy work has been pursued outside the context of improving the inhabitants' standards of living.

Education and leisure

The growth of leisure is one of the salient facts of our time. Whereas, for centuries, leisure was the privilege of one social class, it is tending

126

nowadays to become universal. In an increasing number of countries, workers enjoy shorter working days and working weeks, and several weeks' or even months' holiday a year. Alongside these material and economic factors which govern the use of leisure time, education has a decisive rôle to play. Can it be said that the inhabitants of village and city are prepared, by their education to make the most of the facilities offered them? Experience shows how inadequately people in general are trained or equipped to embark on the great adventure of leisure. This is apparent from their relationship with the resources already available. There may be certain social and cultural facilities missing, but certain facts still cannot be denied: there are few inhabitants of industrialised countries who do not have relatively plentiful cultural resources at their disposal. In France, the United States, and the USSR, for example, there is hardly a household without a television set and one or more radio sets. Setting aside preconceived ideas, one is bound to admit that in the course of a week there are a great many hours when it is possible to tune in to a high quality programme, whether of music, drama, narrative or entertainment. The same is true of films, many of which are not only of great intrinsic interest, but also represent one of the major forms of expression of present-day civilisation. The world's literary classics can now be bought for the price of a packet of cigarettes.

But in fact do we see? The surveys carried out in a great many countries must give us food for thought: the audience for quality programmes is minimal, and where there are several channels, it is automatically the one which puts out the artistically most mediocre and least demanding programmes that commands the widest audience. A kind of civic courage is needed by the programme authorities if they wish to continue to leaven their broadcasting schedules with programmes of an adult character. When they do so, it is in defiance of the taste of the public at large, which has a marked predilection for the stereotyped and the hackneyed, for the uninspired and for candy floss.

In these circumstances, it is unfair to blame the authorities; or to be more exact, the real responsibilities are not at this level but at the level of education and at that very time in a person's life when his tastes, habits and cultural aptitudes are formed. It is at the age of five,

ten or fifteen that one learns to communicate, masters the art of
expression, and discovers the beauty and power of what painting,
poetry and music have to say and that one experiences the revelation
of the tragic and the comic. For the most gifted among us and those
with the greatest staying power, a good start is not so important; to
such as these, moments are sure to come when truth reveals itself, in
spite of obstacles. But for the majority, there is a strong risk of
premature burial of their true being by an education which is content
merely to present models for imitation and which does not aim, first
and foremost, at keeping alive and developing in each individual the
creative instinct and the ability to create.

These thoughts, which were provoked by the behaviour of radio
and television audiences, apply equally well to cinema audiences.
They show the same inability to choose and to gravitate towards what
is best.

What is to be said about reading? It is here that the gulf between the
declared intentions of schooling and its real effects is widest. Surveys
carried out in two Western European countries, France and Italy, have
confirmed our expectations, born of experience: in these countries,
reading is a minority activity. In more than half the households in these
countries no book ever   crosses the threshold. We shall not, at this
point, enter into a discussion of the relative merits of oral and written
communication. All we wish to demonstrate is that an adult who has
spent ten years of his precious existence sitting at a school desk has
perhaps learnt to spell, has perhaps absorbed certain basic rules of
grammar, and knows how long it takes three men to dig two ditches;
but he has not acquired the essential thing that school should have set
out to give him, namely the taste for and habit of reading. Yet books
are the key to almost all serious and profound study and acquisition
of information: outside his own experience, which is necessarily
restricted in space and time, the individual who does not refer to books
has scarcely any means of going beyond the stage of opinion and
building up a coherent body of knowledge. It is also through books
that the individual escapes from the tyranny of the commonplace (and
the sensational) and, rising above events, reaches the stage of reflective
thought and a sense of cultural perspective.

128

If the school does not succeed in raising the individual to this level, it is clearly failing in one of its most imperative tasks — if we accept that the school's purpose is to help men to lead full and worthwhile lives, both at work and in leisure time.

Education and politics

It is also true that politics are not given their proper place in education. Let there be no misunderstanding: I am not referring to political education, which has its time and place depending on one's interests and personal choice, but to education *for* politics. Admittedly, some countries run courses in civics or citizenship, but, as a rule, this is the dullest part of the school curriculum, the part carrying the least conviction and the one to which pupils respond with the blankest indifference. It usually consists of a description of the country's governmental institutions, and a series of lectures on the rights and duties of the citizen. In fact, most pupils reach adulthood without ever having been instructed or encouraged to think about the most important things in their public and private lives: peace, war, justice, social classes and the relations between them, trade unionism, development, and, still more important, the nature, role, functions and structure of the State. The whole of education is weakened by the lack of political consciousness among the greater part of the teaching profession. Nearly all those who are in charge of teaching children see politics as a debased form of human activity, which is unavoidable, but only distantly and indirectly related to culture and the development of the personality. They take the view that once they have 'rendered unto Caesar the things which are Caesar's' by providing courses in civic education, they are then free to attend to their own province, that of the mind.

True enough, the all-round education of the citizen is achieved through other channels as well as formal education. It is by striving for a living wage, for freedom of expression, for his rights, against injustice and by participation and solidarity that the individual develops his political personality and thus becomes adult in the full sense of the word. However, there is often something missing, even among those

129

most determined and competent in political activity: a just, ample and prolonged reflection upon the nature of power, its components, and the forces which act in and through institutions and human beings.

If the purpose of schooling is to prepare people for their life's work and teach them to decipher and understand the structures of the world in which they have to live, so that they do not travel blindly through an incomprehensible universe, and if it is considered important to put a stop to the unhealthy and unjustified separation between the private and the public individual, then the school's task appears in a new light. Priority must be given to educating the individual for democracy. He must be prepared for choice, responsibility, information and participation. It is clear how closely these objectives are connected with the overall objectives of culture, as set out in the foregoing paragraphs. The ability to judge is in fact indivisible, as is the ability to keep oneself informed and to be vigilant.

All educational programmes and methods — at all levels — should be actuated by this concern to awaken political consciousness and develop the virtues of democratic man*. This concern should be made manifest in the content of education. The purpose of teaching literature, history and geography is not merely to stuff the memory with facts and judgements, but to show along what paths the spirit of mankind has journeyed in order to attain self-possession and to learn liberty. There is no finer or more fascinating story, and none reveals so clearly the true meaning of the cultural experience. No discipline is alien to this type of teaching. The role of education for science is, surely, to train minds for research, investigation, discussion, objectivity, risk-taking and intellectual adventure — in short, a set of attitudes and aptitudes which the citizen cannot do without, and which are the firm foundations of any modern democracy. The absence of such political training, from this simultaneously cultural and interdisciplinary angle, is one of the most glaring deficiencies and are of those most fraught with harmful consequences. It constitutes a major obstacle to the development of an adult personality.

---

* The civic virtues which formed the basis of the individual citizen's morality in the *polis* of antiquity have gradually depreciated and given way to the virtues prescribed by a theological and moralistic conception of existence.

The dimensions of the personality

In most educational systems, the models of success and/or failure have been established at a particular moment in the evolution of educational thought and action. For the European (and assimilated) systems, this moment was the heyday of the aristocratic and bourgeois society, i.e., the seventeenth and eighteenth centuries. In those days, the professions which were dominant in influence and prestige were those which used words: churchmen, men of letters, statesmen and administrators, society men (and women), lawyers and magistrates. As a result, the main effort of education was concentrated on instilling the rules and resources of fine language. A flexible and practised memory, stocked with references to the past, and a well-endowed mind, versed in the subtleties of literary invention – these were the important ingredients of success. Society, of which the schools or universities were both the product and the expression, could be relied upon to make good, through its teaching and its rites, whatever education was unable to provide. Continuity was assured between the institution and life as lived. Since then, society has evolved, and conditions, attitudes and customs have changed, but the institution has remained set in old ways.

When it became necessary to provide education for the common people, primary education modelled itself upon the education of the aristocracy – but these were scaled-down models, lacking the spirit which had brought the originals into being (hence it is not surprising that the most vigorous and conscious elements of the working classes failed to find their own image reflected in the values and aims of this kind of education, and looked elsewhere).

Nowadays, the split between the general lines of emphasis of education and the way in which the institutions operate and people's real needs is growing ever wider. Neither the school nor the university is any longer the expression of society as it is, nor are they instruments suited to the development of the personality of people living in the modern world.

The models of success are no longer appropriate – or, at least, if they are suited to anything, it is to reproducing the type of individual who is responsible for putting them into practice, i.e. the teacher. For

131

most people, living conditions are no longer like they were in the past. Work with words has become the exception rather than the rule. Most people nowadays have to come to terms and establish relationships with objects and structures. New dimensions of the personality come into play in defining the human condition and building the future: the dimension of work (and its corollary, leisure), the political dimension which we have discussed above, and also the emotional, artistic and physical dimensions.

Just as education makes an artificial and harmful distinction between culture and politics, so it creates a dangerous separation between mind and body, the emotional and the social. It is aimed at an abstract individual.

Certain philosophers have made much of the taste for the abstract which is so characteristic of education, seeing it as a virtue, and even as the essential virtue of basic education. They have seen in it an instrument for bringing about equality among all men, and hence a source of democracy. Undoubtedly, some equality is introduced by these means; equality in reduction to the abstract mode of being. As it is nevertheless plain to see that there are inequalities in this system — since there are the weak, the strong, the star pupils and those at the bottom of the class — its advocates fall back on a reassuring ideology, namely that of merit, which offers consolation for unjust treatment, teaches resignation to the less gifted and the less successful, and gives a clear conscience to those who come out on top in the competition.

In this so-called order, the advantage goes to those whom nature and the social and cultural circumstances have already favoured. This is the sanctioning of an injustice.

Thus the system commits two fundamental errors: firstly, it overlooks and ignores the complexity of human beings and the multiplicity of natures, temperaments, aspirations, and vocations. This is an act of violence against human nature, and the fact that it occurs at a time in a person's life when he is defenceless and unable to protest makes it all the more serious and inexcusable.

132

SCHOOL AND LIFELONG EDUCATION WITH A VIEW TO BUSINESS MANAGEMENT

Of all the institutions which uphold and assure the functioning of society, it is the school which finds it most difficult to change. The army is seeking new paths and preparations for national defence are now made not in the barracks but in laboratories, in the minds of research workers and in the factories. In all countries, agriculture, albeit the most traditional form of human industry, is taking on a new aspect and undergoing radical structural changes. But schools and education as a whole, with a few notable exceptions, have continued to follow the lines laid down by our forbears of past centuries.

Schools and also, in large measure, universities behave as if we were still living in the age of stagecoach and the salon, of undisputed paternal authority and of women confined to the home. For the school world, capitalist structures have never existed, and work has not become the essential feature of cultural experience; books and the teacher's words still constitute the main, if not the only instruments for the transmission of learning.

This resistance to change is not particularly surprising. Firstly, because one of the functions of education, which must never be overlooked, is to transmit. It devolves on education to maintain the link between present generations and the preceding ones; and however pressing the need to innovate and to follow the evolution of the world, it would be a mistake to break with the past, with the many pasts. What we are today is the product of the work and efforts, the struggles and conquests of countless generations. To ignore this is to understand nothing about ourselves and the world around us; to introduce an element of fragility into the conquests of our time; to deprive ourselves of a fundamental dimension of our age and our destiny, and forgo an endless source of joy.

Thus we can understand, to a certain point, the attitude of those

133

who regard education, and the culture whose instrument it is, as the defence of what they call the cultural heritage. But they are making a fundamental mistake. They forget that this experience of the past and this tradition lose their value and vigour, cease to exist even, except in so far as they form part of the experience of a living individual resolutely committed to the task of forging the destiny of modern man, without reference to a past whose main characteristic is that it no longer exists, and cannot be made to live again, even in thought.

Traditional education is a powerful instrument in the hands of the authorities — authorities of every kind. What the authorities want are docile, obedient people, people who accept meekly and without question the places and roles allotted to them, whether as producers, citizens or elements of the various structures of society; yes-men, prepared to let others think and decide for them, to fall in with the instructions of leaders, guides or heaven-sent men to tell them what to do or not to do, to tell or keep secret, to love or hate, to accept or refuse. In a sense, they live by proxy. Men such as this use the stock replies they have been given and gladly submit to tyranny in all its different forms — the tyranny of fashion, of opinion, of advertising, of collective passions and enthusiasms. In so far as education is the heritage of periods prior to the democratic conception of man and existence, its aims and activities are designed to continue to keep man in a state of protracted infancy and prevent him from becoming adult in the full sense of the word. Education is responsible for the transmission of the ideologies, the frames of reference and the attitudes which set up a screen of prejudice, taboos and ready-made ideas between the reality of the world and the spirit of truth.

If this is the type of man we are aiming at — someone who has no mind of his own and whose ideas, tastes and decisions are imposed from without — then there is no reason to make any substantial changes in the present situation. Traditional education has a kind of perfection, and is absolutely logical. There is no need to assume any ill-will in explanation of the attitudes of most of the people responsible for education: they quite naturally maintain a system favourable to them and expressing the vision of man and the world with which they themselves, under this system, have been impregnated. They are in perfectly good faith, for instance, when they believe in the ideology of merit, for they fail to see that the so-called merit of the clever pupils, who have triumphed over the less clever, in fact conceals such flagrant and inordinate injustices as the privilege of birth or money.

But this system, so perfect of its kind, so solidly entrenched in established interest and prejudices, is now beginning to be seriously challenged. Searching questions about the justification of existing procedures are no new phenomena. In the past two centuries, proposals for reform have been made by all the major schools of thought, from the time of Rousseau to that of the existentialists and including Hegel, Nietsche and, in our day, Piaget, all of whom have called in question the theory and practice of our educational system. But it is only in the past few years that protest has extended outside learned works and the specialist's study. It is to be found, today, everywhere: in the streets and the universities, in the minds and hearts of thousands, if not millions, of young people, whose protest represents that combination of folly and wisdom peculiar to their age. They are sometimes reproached with being confused in their ideas. People say of them: 'They don't know what they want. It's easy enough to pull things down, but you must know what to put up in their place.' The important point is that they express their views, their perplexity, their concern, in many cases their misfortunes, with force. They protest against a system based on injustice, lack of respect for man, the utilisation of talent by an inhuman society, the triumph of the strong and the lucky and the condemnation of the weak. That certain suspect elements take the opportunity to express their spirit of destruction and nihilism is no justification for remaining deaf to this appeal.

This movement, essentially revolutionary and instinctive, coincides with the reflections and conclusions of a whole group of specialists belonging to a wide variety of disciplines: the psychologists, who denounce the damage done by a system of education concentrating on a syllabus and caring nothing for the pupils, who are subjected to a random process of selection; the sociologists, who show up the structure of education as archaic and retrograde; the economists, who maintain that the money spent on education gives poor returns and that human resources are wasted; and the philosophers, who take the

135

view that education in its present form serves to divert people from their real vocation, which is to accept man's estate, live it to the full and reveal the true nature of man by a process of education which continues throughout his life.

A first series of questions relates to the age when education takes place. Traditionally, life was divided into two periods: a period of preparation which was comparatively short, since it coincided with childhood and adolescence; and a period of practical activity, much longer, in that it lasted until the end of a man's days. The two periods were separated by a series of ceremonies similar to the initiation rites of primitive societies: examinations and, for the privileged, the award of diplomas. This kind of separation, though in itself artificial, could still be maintained at the time when societies were stable, that is to say when they were still dominated by an agrarian-type civilisation. Until fairly recently, the images and character of the world in which a man completed his existence differed little from those of the world into which he was born; and most people could acquire in their early years sufficient knowledge and ability for self-expression to carry them through safely to the end of their alloted span. Continuity between the two worlds, that of life and that of school, was assured. What education lacked, society provided: traditions, customs, the lessons and the example of the older generations, opinions and pressures of the environment. People went through life progressing from stage to stage, finally completing the cycle, after playing all the standard parts of adulthood, by donning the garb of the old.

But what a very different picture life now presents. A whole new civilisation lies between the cradle and the grave. The physical, moral and intellectual scene of our lives changes radically, not merely from one generation to the next, but sometimes even from year to year. Modern nations are no longer the countries of twenty years ago. Whole regions are being emptied of their active populations, which go to swell the populations of the towns. The development of industries and the increase of incomes has been accompanied by the installation of a consumer society in which the young have become prime movers. It is unnecessary to stress the extent to which morals and manners have changed — in all sections of society. You yourselves have watched this

136

happen, are witness to the fact that no one has escaped these changes. But there are also other things more serious, and still more decisive. For centuries, whole sections of our populations have lived, intellectually and spiritually, on firm, stable, unequivocal interpretations of a set of beliefs and certitudes. Admittedly, these beliefs and certitudes still exist. They are firmly rooted. But what a difference between now and the situation only twenty years ago! For each of the major faiths from which men draw their support and inspiration there are today multiple interpretations and many schools of thought. To allow oneself to be guided, step by step, by a teacher of uncontestable, uncontested authority is becoming less and less possible. Every individual is now obliged to choose, so that choice is, for all of us, central to our experience. It would even seem that we are, so to speak, driven to independence, forced to be free. Even in that section of science which seemed to be furthest removed from the threat of storms and eruptions — mathematics — we are now witnessing strange upheavals. Teachers of this discipline, who would be capable of speaking more learnedly of this phenomenon, will bear me out. And as to physics and chemistry and their applications to industry, agriculture and medicine, here again we are in a state of flux, constantly making new discoveries. Countless professions are affected by this acceleration of change, making it essential to go on adding constantly to our knowledge or techniques.

It is no longer possible, in these conditions, to speak of cultural or intellectual qualifications. The knowledge and know-how accumulated in any one period of life quickly becomes out of date, and loses its value. Anyone nowadays who desires to keep up to date and in touch with developments is obliged to engage constantly in 'refresher' training, to use a term with which you are familiar, as much on the social plane as on that of general and professional education.

This is an indication of the importance of the part played by adult education. Since the education people receive in childhood and adolescence no longer suffices to enable them to lead a satisfactory life, adults cannot afford not to go on training, studying and acquiring new skills. This is difficult to do, people will say. Adults have little time; they are tired, taken up by all manner of worries and responsibilities. There is no doubt some truth in these objections. But

137

the economic difficulties often alleged are largely imaginary; and in fact, adults in our societies have much more spare time than they are willing to admit. Think only of all the hours spent in cafés, watching television or reading rubbishy magazines. Adults who are said to be exhausted are in fact capable of making great efforts, provided they have the interest or desire to do so.

Then there is another factor which plays a decisive part in our age – the increase of leisure. After being for generations the privilege of a small minority, leisure has now become available to millions of workers, bringing a new dimension into their lives. It is reckoned that, before long, people in our societies will devote much more time to rest and recreation than they do to their work. This raises the major question of what they are to do with their leisure. The answer lies partly in education. The first point is that there must be education for leisure, that is to say that people must be prepared and trained to make worthy use of this free time. And secondly, provision must be made for education during leisure time. That is to say that a large proportion of people's spare evenings and weekends, and also of their weeks and months of holiday could and should be used for intellectual activities, study and research, occupations designed to arouse their curiosity and involving the pursuit of all kinds of artistic activities. This is in any case the only way of making sure that leisure becomes an asset, and not a source of boredom and estrangement.

What, in these conditions, is the place and the role of the school? I put this question to those of you whose job it is to teach children. I think you will agree that the role of education, whilst decreasing in one sense, will increase in another. If education extends to the whole of life, the school will occupy a comparatively short period in relation to the process as a whole. The time for education in the full sense of the word will be in adult life, when man is in a position to play both an objective and a subjective role in his own education. The school will then constitute rather an important, decisive prelude to the full and complete process of education.

But at the same time the responsibility devolving on school education will increase considerably, since it will be directed to the development of the person as a whole, instead of concentrating, as

138

hitherto, on the transmission of knowledge.

You may well ask at this juncture what I understand by education. My reply will be at once simple in its wording and complex in its implications: education is the development of the human being, by the exploitation of his capacities in all the variety of his experience. This definition is probably incomplete but I doubt, in view of the complexity of the elements involved, whether a wholly satisfactory definition can be found. At all events, this formula takes account of the following points.

The accent is on the *human being*. The real education process concentrates not on a body of knowledge designated arbitrarily as the content of education, but on the needs of the human being, his aspirations and the living relations he maintains with the world of objects and persons. Education covers everything that can provide intellectual, aesthetic or spiritual sustenance for the individual and becomes an integral part of his being. To put it the other way round, the content of any teaching, whatever its importance or value, is educationally worthless if it remains external, if it is not adapted to the recipient's abilities and reactions. Life, with its needs, conditions, rhythms and expressions, is therefore to be regarded as our supreme guide in all our educational ventures.

The accent is also on *development*. For this human being of whom we are speaking is not what he is for one day or one moment, but during the whole of his existence. He is what he does and what he becomes at every moment of his life, at every stage of his development, with all his achievements, failings and successes judged, superseded and assimilated. For him, the truth is not a given fact but has to be conquered. As we can see from so many examples of the work of artists, it is at the end of the road and not at the beginning, after passing through many different stages, that a man really comes into his own, provided that at the start he has not been cut off from the sources of creativity.

Placing the accent on the human being also means placing it on the importance of differences. No two beings are identical. Each has his own originality, his special characteristics and his own way of living his life, even if he resembles others. It is precisely through his specificity,

139

provided that it is respected, that he can attain the universality of man's estate and true fraternity with his fellow men.

One conclusion stands out, namely that there is no one education, but as many educational processes as there are individuals. It is of prime importance to individualise education at all levels, whether one is dealing with adults or with young people and children.

If education caters for the human being, then it must cater for the human being as a whole — including the intellectual aspect, of course, but the other aspects are just as important, although they are usually neglected or forgotten. Sensibility, like the mind, can be trained, and this is equally necessary. The ability and desire to communicate with others must also be taken care of. These are the essential bases of sociability. The same is true of the various outlets for artistic instinct, whether in music or in the visual arts. Emotional, social and artistic illiteracy are as great a threat to the balance of the individual, and ultimately of society, as the other forms of illiteracy which are better known and easier to identify. The unilateral development of cognitive intelligence, at the expense of other modes of perceiving reality and controlling the resources of one's personality produces psychologically distorted people who are unable to live in this world with the necessary ease, competence and grace. Even more so when it comes to the human body, which for centuries and even nowadays has been and is the first thing to be forgotten in the educational process. 'Know your body' is the title of a number of a would-be-spiritualist journal. This is indeed a priority objective today — to know one's body in order to master it, to exploit its powers of expression and communication and to curb its excesses. For there is physical degradation, but is it not attended by intellectual and emotional degradation? Balance is the key word here, with care for every dimension of our being and the support that each dimension can give to the others.

Can any education worthy of the name fail to take these requirements into account? Now, you know the situation. How many limits and constraints are imposed by educational structures and by the tyranny of traditional curricula and methods? Is it not true that the objectives of school education should be thoroughly re-examined, so as to take into account all facets of the personality and differences of

140

nature, temperament, aspirations and natural bents? With the present rigid system, only those who, through their temperament and ability to adapt their talents, are able to conform to the prevailing models can profit by it. The others become marginal or take refuge in dreams, or else in the comfortable and reassuring, but finally traumatising, position of the bad pupil.

Rather than using the term curriculum, which always suggests something rigid and fixed, let us speak of content and trends. These are indicated by an analysis of requirements, such as that made above, but which naturally changes according to the transformations occurring in the lives of individuals and of societies. It may also be noted that a balance should always be struck between the requirements of the community and those of the individual; and this is often a difficult task.

This twofold, complementary reference to the developing human being and to life has one major consequence. It is abundantly clear that education is at work in many different situations and circumstances, wherever people are learning, acquiring knowledge, training themselves and shaping their personality. In other words, education goes on in a job, in the life of a couple, in relations between parents and children (a two-way process, incidentally, if it be true that parents have as much to learn from their children as vice versa). This has always been the case, but, today, it has become an urgent and often crucial reality. It is to be seen in full force in different civic, political or trade union commitments. It is scarcely possible to become an adult without taking an active part in the various forms of national life. Needless to say, these situations are of course all ambivalent and ambiguous. They may form or deform the character. Hence the importance of habits and attitudes, the foundations of which are laid in the first years of life. As you may imagine, this is not in any way an attempt to diminish the importance of the part played by the school, but to shed light as well on the overriding, fundamental importance of the education received within the family.

We now come to the great problem of *methods*, which is central to our subject, since it concerns the human being. Method is know-how, habit, reflexes and organisation. It is the ambition of every teacher worthy of the name to develop and implant firmly in his pupils the

141

ability to learn and to evolve, as well as a taste for intellectual work, exercise and training, without which there is no true education.

If we accept this viewpoint, it is our right and, indeed, our duty to ask whether all these methods which are available to us, these traditional techniques, this bag of tricks inherited from the past, thanks to which we continue to educate generations of pupils, are adapted to our purposes? Can we continue to use mechanisms which have the effect of causing large sectors of each generation to lose faith in the educational system, to such a point that they will never again take part in any form of education? Can we continue to run on the same lines an educational system whose avowed and concealed percentages of failure are higher than those of any other human enterprise? Who would accept the idea that an engineer should construct bridges, with the expectation that one out of two, or two out of three, would collapse as soon as traffic passed over them? And yet it does not strike us as scandalous — because we are so used to it — that men should be held in less regard than stones and animals. Wars, revolutions, and the exploitation of the workers, testify to this. Education is another example, although more subtle and better disguised. The moment has come to show that we are scandalised. It is a matter of urgency to remedy the situation and put an end to wastage which costs society so much and ruins so many careers.

As soon as it is realised that it is a question of helping men to live, the rules of a new methodology follow automatically:

To put the emphasis on the *pupil* and not on the curriculum. This follows on logically from the foregoing premisses.

To consider education as a process and not as the transmission of knowledge.

To substitute qualitative appreciation of the child as an individual for quantitative assessment which establishes artificial scales between individuals.

To reduce *competition* to a minimum and replace it by a system of team-work to which each brings his own talents and personal experience and contributes to the common search for knowledge through his curiosity and his questions.

To treat children as children, with the problems of their age and not as miniature adults. The more a child lives a full and harmonious childhood and, as an adolescent, a true adolescence, the better prepared he will be for adult life. Otherwise he will always look back with regret and nostalgia upon a ruined childhood.

To judge as little as possible, for judgement halts and betrays an existence.

To link education to life as far as possible. This means, *inter alia*, preparation for a working life and preparation for leisure. It seems to me that it is just as important to use radio, television and films in school, as it is to teach children to understand a tragedy by Corneille.

Children should be taught in these early years to choose and recognise what is good and useful as opposed to what is bad and harmful. It is through intelligent practice that they will learn how to behave properly and not through speeches or sermons.

The same reasoning applies to *information*. The children of today are the citizens of tomorrow. They must be trained, as from now, to abstract from the knowledge imparted and the messages addressed to them genuine information, based on critical judgement and a scientific approach.

These are only a few examples of the link between education and the situations with which life faces us. Each will find others for himself.

The time has come for all teachers to acquire an *extensive, sound* knowledge of the basic principles of psychology, characterology, and group and environmental sociology which will enable them to understand each of the pupils entrusted to their care. Educators must no longer be more or less gifted transmitters of knowledge, but rather technicians of the personality. For this they need knowledge, but also practical experience and art. This is required of technicians of the body such as doctors. Can we ask less of a technician of the intellectual, emotional and spiritual aspects of human nature?

Although all the foregoing reflections apply to the general run of situations, they are clearly relevant first and foremost to the business world.

Traditional education still prepares future adults as if human activity consisted mainly of rhetoric. For in the seventeenth and eighteenth

143

centuries, when the structures of secondary education were established, as was pointed out earlier the professions dominant in both power and prestige were those connected with the mastery of words, that is to say, lawyers, churchmen, men of letters, soldiers and politicians. Other occupations were marginal and left to the random workings of experience and improvisation. The world has changed. Social functions and hierarchies have been modified but the spirit of the school and the university has remained, *mutatis mutandis*, basically the same.

What modern society needs at all levels is a different kind of man and therefore a new kind of education. The individual today must be equipped to cope with the real, concrete tasks of the modern world which are first and foremost economic and technical. This is bound to entail radical and substantial changes in the objectives, curricula and methods at the various levels of education.

What is of prime importance is to reconcile culture and work. If it be true that genuine culture reflects man's efforts to transform all the features of Nature in order to give them a human face and character, then clearly those who are engaged in production are the most powerful instruments of this human intervention in the natural order. This is what all teachers in our schools have forgotten and continue to overlook. They see human life as divided into two parts. One part is concerned with freedom, pleasure, and nobility of spirit, dedicated to literature, the arts and theoretical science. According to their way of thinking, this is the cultural part of life. The other part is focused on the need to earn a living, with the shrunken personality turning its back on culture. This, they say, is the fate of human labour in all its forms. Nothing could be further from the truth, for there are no such divisions of the human personality. As for cultural experience, nothing could be further from the truth either, for it embraces all aspects of human life, and professional activity to begin with. It is high time that educators became aware of these fundamental facts in modern society which put the structures and development of the individual and social personality in true perspective.

Next, the essential task of modern education will be to prepare men for change. The spirit of adventure, risk, research, experiment and renewal, which is the essence of science and of historical evolution,

144

must penetrate deeply into the structures and curricula of our educational systems. It is no longer a question of revealing knowledge, whatever it may be, but of equipping everyone, by appropriate means, so that he can pursue his own investigation. If I am not mistaken, this is the kind of man, with his feet firmly on the ground, realistic in the philosophical and methodological sense of the word, who can ensure the successful operation of our societies, industrial, commercial and administrative structures.

This is the kind of man who is produced by lifelong education. If he has been suitably trained from childhood, he will never cease to learn, to study and thus to educate himself. He will never think that he has reached a point of knowledge or perfection which allows him to stop. But always, tirelessly, he will test his knowledge against facts and changing situations, while at the same time, playing his part in the building of a more harmonious and just world, less wasteful of human resources.

This surely also means that business management cannot be considered as an end in itself independently of the other aspects of the life of societies and individuals. The aims of management must coincide with the general aims of society and take into account the basic aspirations of people in the world today.

Those responsible for business administration must not forget that they, too, are citizens, just like other people, even if they have more power and heavier responsibility. It is in so far as the fact of sharing a common nature and a common destiny with all mankind is grasped and reflected in practice that business management can assume its profound significance, which is to serve men and not an abstract and sterile image of success.

STONES AND MEN

The human body is not made of flesh and bone alone. It is also made of stones. For it is in the stones of the house, the street and the town that this collective self, in which we all play a part and through which we all, willy-nilly, express ourselves, settles and develops. It receives a large part of its conceptions and feelings and even of its perceptions from the material substratum of its existence.

What lessons in living and behaviour are received by the average human being whose life is spent in a modern housing estate or a block of flats, or one whose childhood and youth were passed among the houses of suburbia? They were lessons in isolation, distrust and restriction, with communication denied and no contact with others. The individual self becomes a special possession whose keys and secrets are kept snugly concealed from the outside world. This is the language of doors, bolts, railings and watch dogs; this is the eternal refrain of the narrow passages and closed doors — housing the machines in which the death of a neighbour is learnt from scanning the obituary columns in the newspaper.

This is how most people in our modern societies spend their lives. They live in prison — the prison of their room, their flat, their means of transport, their office or factory, their small, apportioned task, the prison of their individual consciousness turned in on itself and immured in its precious intimacy.

Is not the place where a child is introduced to knowledge and where he spends the greater part of his youth itself a kind of prison? Here, he is deprived of his liberty, has tasks imposed on him, must submit to the decisions of an all-powerful teacher whose business it is to judge him unremittingly. Added to this, school buildings are, with a few exceptions, modelled, both inside and out, on erections for the incarceration of adults, namely prisons or barracks.

What a contrast between this language of things and the language of

146

men! The primary and secondary school teachers speak to us of universalism. Through them, although distorted and hardly recognisable, come the messages of the poets, the inventors of stories and legends, and explorers of the outer and inner worlds. These are lessons of fellowship and brotherhood. The schoolmaster's words conjure up the picture of a united human race. The priest and vicar also talk of our common destiny. They speak of love and reconciliation. But, once out of church, this 'neighbour' of whom they spoke turns out to be the man next to us in the tube whose smell or appearance we cannot endure.

We must not, of course, expect that a transformation of the material framework of life will solve everything. We must not imagine that we shall have radiant cities and houses, so long as the economic and social structures of life stay as they are. The conflict between languages mirrors the conflict between classes and sectors. The chaos visible in the building of our towns and homes reflect the chaos of civilisation. It is the same contempt for the human elements that governs the anarchic utilisation of the labour force and the building of homes. If we wish to have done with building chaos, whatever the scale on which it occurs, it is imperative that we work towards a new order in industry and human relations. The civilisation of a country or of an age is an indivisible phenomenon and it is utopian to imagine a harmonious material world which is built, lived in and inspired by lost souls.

Does this mean that nothing is possible and that nothing must be dared until the great events which are to change the face of the earth come to pass? This is what some people think and one can see why. But it is a short-sighted view. The history of the last fifty years has confirmed — if there was any need for it — that although civilisation is indivisible and although the temporal and the spiritual are firmly linked, the various elements do not proceed at the same pace.

Some countries have had their economic revolution but have maintained the traditional framework of authority and power. Even where socialism has been established and where the class system has been abolished, there has been a lack of imagination in creating material frameworks for life to match the new ideology. The daily round for workers varies little from one industrial society to another, whether

147

this society be red, pink or verging on white. One single and very important exception is the development of community leisure-time structures. There are large numbers of libraries, sports grounds, young pioneers' clubs and cultural centres in the Soviet Union and, generally speaking, in all those countries which follow or try to follow its example.

There is another thing which reduces the temptation to demand all or nothing. Whilst it is true that the material environment cannot have a human character or aspect until men themselves have become fully human in a spirit of reconciliation and communication, it is equally true that this will not occur by magic. The great decisive changes will come about only if the way is paved for them by a multitude of half-way changes serving a two-fold purpose: firstly to provide particular solutions to particular problems and, secondly, to prepare, in co-operation with others, for major overall reforms. Each innovation, whether in art, music, morals and customs, or the status of men and women, has this dual significance. It is the same for education.

It is becoming increasingly clear that education can no longer follow the paths blazed for it by age-old traditions. Current systems and practices which restrict men's education to childhood and youth and which perpetuate the objectives and methods of our forefathers without reference to the way in which people really live or to the diversity of human nature, are proving, more and more, to be erroneous, ineffective and unjust. The research and thinking of psychologists, sociologists and economists and the experience of the most perceptive educators lead to the same conclusion, namely that education must be considered as a continuous process going on throughout one's life and every stage of one's development. The consequences of taking this stand are limitless. Everything must be reviewed and thought out afresh: the structures of education, the place, rôle and content of curricula, the objectives of primary education, the links and relationships between the different forms of education at the various ages (childhood, adolescence, maturity and old age), the recruitment, rôle and training of teachers, etc.

Nevertheless, all those engaged in this task of renewing instruction and training in the context of lifelong education are fully aware of the

148

obstacles and contradictions existing in the institutional, legal, economic and material frameworks of life. What is the good of teaching men to communicate and to be forthcoming with each other if they live in a world of walls and barriers? What is the good of teaching them to express themselves and to reveal themselves both to themselves and to others through theatre, singing, drawing, or sport if they have neither places where they can meet nor the instruments of these various incarnations of the poetic instinct?

It is thus unthinkable that educators should find themselves alone in their search for new forms of education. They have no chance of succeeding unless, from the outset, they establish a strong, living alliance with all those responsible for building towns and houses, that is to say, with political and administrative authorities, town planners, architects, builders, etc. Inversely, and for the same reasons, is it not vital for these people who are concerned with building to co-operate with and be constantly available to all those who can tell them about the needs (continuing and/or peculiar to our times) of individuals, groups and societies? This is certainly one of the most patent manifestations of the indivisible nature of efforts to civilise the world.

CONVERSATION WITH THE AUTHOR

Q. Amongst the short-term of objectives of a lifelong education policy, you propose measures to develop adult education structures. Why give preference to adults?
A. Because adult education, seen in the context of lifelong education, is the 'locomotive'.

There are several things to explain this. First of all, we can point to the fact that reason and common sense do not make any headway through their own merits. History shows, for example, that what has brought about desirable progress in the status of workers, women and young people is not reason but the impatience and revolt of those concerned. A child at school may feel ill at ease or even unhappy. He can express his uneasiness by making a nuisance of himself but he is not equipped to rebel because he has not had the adult's experience of independence. Children do not themselves think how education should be improved. The ones who do this are the adults. Adult education would therefore appear to be a decisive factor for the maturation of the whole process.

Another thing is that modern educational theory stresses the idea of independence and of teaching pupils to be self-reliant. The idea is not a new one, of course, but it has the virtue of providing some solution to the problem of the present-day clash of ideologies which is leaving individuals and communities alike with no firm ground to stand on. Now, to be independent is to be an adult. The true subject of education is also the adult. For the educational dialogue can only be initiated on the basis of questions arising out of experience of life (e.g. professional, family and social life). Children, on the other hand, have education thrust upon them, at least in our present system where education does not represent the answers to any interrogation.

With regard to the cost of the nation's educational investments,

150

adult education is a way of recovering part of these non-productive investments. For in so far as the selection system forces out people who have nevertheless been educated, retrieving them as adults compensates for the amount spent on them while they were at school.

Lastly, in a more general way, education is going further and further beyond its function of transmitting the values of a society. As a means of production, human faculties – or in other words the general level of education – play just as important a part as any other form of capital. This is the context in which adult education fulfils one of its main roles. Another thing is that it brings quicker returns than school education since it makes it possible to equip the most active and go-ahead people in a district or region to become the agents of development.

Q. You say that lifelong education can help to remedy one of the most critical situations in modern society – that arising out of the generation gap. How can lifelong education contribute here?
A. It is quite obvious that not all the problems involved in the present crisis in the relations between young people and adults can be solved by educational means. For example, the resentment of the system shown by students is mainly due to lack of confidence in their career prospects. It is a problem of investment, of the organisation of labour and, in the last resort, of social structures and the political régime. This amounts, in fact, to a series of political measures, but they are not foreign to education since they must be inspired by a conception of mankind and the establishment of structures which make access to higher forms of cultural life possible and easy.

But these relations will develop in different ways and in a new style if the spirit of lifelong education spreads among adults.

No one will deny the necessity for the regular transmission of knowledge and experience from the adult world to the young. You cannot re-invent everything with every generation, but if this knowledge and experience are to remain transmittable, there must be a new mode of communication. No adult message will henceforth be accepted if it is conveyed in an authoritarian fashion, as a truth deriving its strength from the superior position of one person in relation to the other, whether father, teacher or official. If, however, the elder (whoever he may be) places himself on the same footing as the younger, if his sole desire is to engage with him in the joint pursuit of knowledge, then all communication becomes possible. The adoption of a scientific approach and the sincere and frank acceptance of the relativity of judgements and opinions can alone lead to reconciliation and real communication between people of different ages. Moreover, what I feel to be true of the youth-adult relationship might be equally true of communication between all categories of human beings whose relationship is that of dominant-dominated, e.g. men and women, men of different races, or developed and developing countries. As for the young, they might ponder the relativity of their situation and the fact that youth is a temporary state which must, of course, be lived to the full and without reservation, but that the normal term of this exceptional period of life is adulthood, and that to become adult in the full sense is an aim for which it is worth striving with all the fire and resolve they can command.

Q. You make lifelong education a prerequisite for the democratic development of society. How do you explain this?
A. It is because it is the instrument of equality. For the desire for equality is a deep-rooted instinct in most men. Willy-nilly and whether he be aware of it or not, every man bears the burdens of the whole human race and when he finds himself belittled, despised or humiliated by reason of his status, the whole human race is stricken through him and protests and demands the restoration of his dignity. This, of course, is a demand for justice, but the attempt to establish equality leads far beyond that. It aims at nothing less than creating or re-creating the conditions in which we are or become 'fellow-men'. I see no need to go into the rôle of the capitalist system here. Through the interplay of its forces and the effects of its contradictions, it has done a great deal to destroy this human 'fellow-ship'. We have all become enemies. Thanks to the law of competition between individuals, different circles, clans and classes, men no longer recognise themselves in the destiny of their fellow-men.

The ways in which modern man is trying to restore this ruined

152

fellowship are many and varied, and largely complementary. Through improved organisation of labour, increased productivity, rational planning and technical innovations, industrial society is steadily adding to the resources which enable it to lessen the gap between the living conditions of the privileged and the under-privileged. Every year, there are fewer and fewer people condemned by poverty to live at starvation level.

The same can be said of the beneficial effects (from the point of view of equality, practical justice and the re-creation of conditions for the recognition of our 'fellow-men') of the various aspects of social demands. In its strong desire for a better life and in its instinctive or conscious will to destroy capitalism's harmful effects, the working class is striving for the overall good of mankind.

But this action at the level of production and distribution, however necessary and fraught with cultural values it may be, fosters an illusion — which is to believe that it will suffice for the re-establishment of a human order. It is, in fact, only one of the two keys to the solution. The second key is education. Education is called upon to play a part in modern society which is unparalleled in any earlier period. It would seem that up till now, education has existed in a pre-historic state and is only now assuming its historic rôle, in that man, through new conceptions and in new ways, is destined to become the priority subject of his own education and no longer, as in the past, to have education thrust upon him. Education has, of course, already acted as a very powerful equaliser in the past. Everyone knows what the school has done not only to teach the rudiments (and more) but to instil into every individual common points of reference and the myths and mythologies on which a national community is based.

It has nevertheless contributed just as forcibly towards destroying the conditions for the recognition of our 'fellow-men'. It has institutionalised differences between us. It has established competition as the law governing relations between people. In the school system, each pupil is put on a particular rung of a ladder above one category of pupils and below another. At school (if one discounts the regulatory and corrective effect of natural affinities) everyone is already heading towards a state of hostility.

153

This hostility is strengthened by the tyranny of the models used for instruction and the moulding of minds. These models, inherited from bygone ages, are doubly oppressive. First of all they have been worked out over the centuries and their rightness has never really been questioned. Secondly, they are based on a truncated idea of human nature which includes only the intellectual (or rather cognitive) aspect of the individual and disregards the other aspects (or harmonic components). Those who are adapted to these models by temperament and natural bent do not suffer unduly from them. They see in the approved curricula and methods and extension, a mirror, as it were, of their own personality. Since this adaptation gives them a natural superiority in academic competition, these are the ones who, through the workings of elimination and competition, as a rule become the masters of the system and the callers of the tune. The rest, whose characters are formed and assert themselves in other ways, are relegated to the fringe. This leads to lack of balance, tensions and failures. It is one of the factors which most assuredly increases inequality in our society, all the more so in that it goes under the glittering guise of merit.

In lifelong education, on the other hand, everyone finds his own road to development since it offers a series of different kinds of education and training which cater for each one's individuality, originality and calling.

Here we come back to what I said to start with. In a modern society, where poverty is no longer oppressive and where the material conditions of life are tending to become uniform, lifelong education may be regarded as the instrument of true equality.

As the notion of lifelong education takes root and influences structures and institutions, the artificial differences between men will tend to disappear, yielding place to the real difference which is what distinguishes one man from another, each having his own logic, his unmistakable originality and his particular calling to follow. When an individual no longer sees the success of another as preventing his own success, then a great barrier to communication will have been lifted. Through lifelong education, man's natural aggressiveness will find its normal outlet. The aim of such education is not to incite the individual

154

to destroy his 'rival' but to carry on the war which every man must wage in himself and with himself. Lifelong education is an encouragement to everyone to fight a never-ending battle against prejudice, ready-made ideas, dead conventions, stereotypes and the successive crystallisations of existence. In this, such education comes uncommonly close to life, following its rhythms, heeding its lessons and blazing its trails.

As an individual frees himself from false competition, he comes to rely on his refound fellow-man who has the same problems as himself, in whom he recognises the same humanity and who has the same aims in life. Here true equality, the specific equality of man's estate, coincides with true freedom or rather the process of liberation whereby man, throughout his life, gets to know himself, provided he is not afraid to face the truth as he sees it, and has the necessary strength, which he will draw mainly from exchange and alliance with his fellow-men.

Q. Do you not think that lifelong education is a luxury which developing countries cannot afford?
A. We have often heard this said in the Third World. Those in charge of education in those countries are aware of the ever-increasing burden of education on the national economy. In many cases, expenditure has reached a ceiling beyond which it is impossible to go without endangering financial equilibrium and the normal functioning of the economy. When we talk to them of lifelong education, the spectre of fresh expenditure immediately looms before their eyes. It is easy to understand why they are not very keen.

But this fear, which appears justified at first sight, is unfounded when examined more closely. For what really is the point at issue? Not necessarily to add new pieces to a pre-existing whole, but to bring order out of chaos. These people in charge are the first to admit that their schools and universities by no means meet their people's real needs today. In many cases and in many respects, education in its present forms is a hindrance to development. If lifelong education intimates and reflects a desire to adapt education to situations and resources, then there is no reason for them to be afraid of it; on the contrary, they

155

should draw inspiration from this concept and give priority to its application in practice. Is it not even more vital for societies of this type to avoid the ruinous waste caused by the traditional system? The luxury that these countries cannot afford is precisely to invest in training and educating a proportion of the population, only to see those who have been educated reverting to ignorance or incompetence.

Q. Then you would like adults in developing countries to go back to school?
A. Not at all. That is where the mistake, the misinterpretation, lies. It is not even certain that schools in their present form should be maintained for children. But we must find new ways, adapted to local conditions, in order to guarantee the constant dissemination of essential notions and the acquisition of techniques and know-how. Lifelong education therefore means — here as elsewhere — an attempt at coherence, a mobilisation of available resources and manpower and new lines of thought in education.